Speaking Solutions

P9-DXN-051

Speaking Solutions

Interaction, Presentation, Listening, and Pronunciation Skills

Candace Matthews
The George Washington University
Washington, D.C.

Contributor:
Phillip Edmondson
The George Washington University

Drawings by Paul Stephen Docksey

Longman

Library of Congress Cataloging-in-Publication Data

Matthews, Candace
    Speaking solutions : interaction, presentation, listening, and pronunciation
skills / Candace Matthews ; contributor, Phillip Edmondson ; drawings by
Paul Stephen Docksey.
        p. cm.
    ISBN 0–13–701229–2
    1. English language—Textbooks for foreign speakers. 2. English language—
Spoken English. 3. English language—Pronunciation. 4. Conversation.
5. Listening. I. Edmondson, Phillip. II. Title.
PE1128.M3543   1994
428.3'4—dc20

93–45923
CIP

Credits: Pages 32 (top two photos), 160, 195: Laima Druskis. Pages 35, 165: Laimute E.
Druskis. Pages 38, 45: Ken Karp. Page 55: American Red Cross photo by Rudolph
Vetter. Pages 82, 115: Eugene Gordon. Pages 86, 148: AP/Wide World Photos. Page
114: Charles Gatewood. Pages 120, 187: A.T.&T. Co. Photo Center. Page 138: 3M's
Audio Visual Division. Page 180 (left): Shirley Zeiberg. All other photos courtesy of
the author.

Acquisitions editor: Nancy Baxer
Copy editor: Sherry Babbitt
Editorial/production supervision: Peggy Gordon
Cover designer: Tom Nery
Production coordinator: Ray Keating

© 1994 by Prentice Hall Regents
Pearson Education
10 Bank Street
White Plains, NY 10606

All rights reserved. No part of this book may be
reproduced, in any form or by any means,
without permission in writing from the publisher.

Printed in the United States of America

30 29 28 27 26 25 24 23   V056   11 12 13

ISBN 0-13-701229-2

In memory of two dear friends,
Don Henderson and Ralph Hosmer

Contents

Preface

Purpose

The purpose of *Speaking Solutions: Interaction, Presentation, Listening, and Pronunciation Skills* is to develop the oral communication skills of intermediate through advanced ESL/EFL students in academic and professional settings. The text is intended for use in pre-academic college classes, intensive ESL/EFL programs, private language schools, and English training courses for professionals. It is designed to be covered in one semester but is easily adaptable to other periods of time.

The interactive activities in the text involve learners in practicing skills that they can apply to real-life situations. Promoting cumulative learning, *Speaking Solutions* helps students:

- Participate successfully in conversations and small group discussions
- Plan, organize, and deliver effective presentations by following clear, specific guidelines
- Improve listening and pronunciation skills by doing activities based on an accompanying audiotape
- Strengthen critical thinking skills by brainstorming, supporting opinions, considering values, making decisions, solving problems, and analyzing issues
- Analyze the effectiveness of discussions and presentations by using a variety of self, peer, and group observation forms
- Gain sensitivity to basic cross-cultural issues
- Take responsibility for their own learning by doing a variety of learner-training activities

Format

Unit 0 has a unique format featuring introductory activities. These activities are designed to help students get to know one another and to feel comfortable speaking English in class. Then, Units 1 through 7 have basically the same format. Each unit opens with a page of photographs and discussion questions to encourage students to share their ideas and opinions with one another in an informal way. You may put students in pairs or in small groups to discuss the answers to the questions and then share ideas as a class. The rest of each unit is divided into sections:

Listening Practice. This section includes task-based listening activities based on an accompanying audiotape. These activities focus on the functions, skills, and strategies presented in the Communication Skills section of the unit. It is important for the teacher to review these activities in advance in order to decide whether to use each activity to **introduce** a particular skill or to **reinforce** the skill after covering it in the Communication Skills section. In many cases, students may need to listen to each activity several times in order to focus on both content and language use.

Communication Skills. The information presented in this section focuses on specific conversation, discussion, or presentation skills. The activities are generally self-explanatory, with students expressing opinions, making decisions, solving problems, planning presentations, and so forth. This section also includes lists of expressions used to convey different language functions, such as agreeing, disagreeing, and asking for clarification in order to help students expand their knowledge of English. The expressions listed are limited to common examples that are appropriate in academic and professional situations. Of course, it is not possible to list all possible expressions for each function, so you may want to add to the lists as you work through each unit.

Pronunciation Practice. The activities in this section, based on the audiotape, focus on stress, rhythm, and intonation.

Learning Strategies. Learner-training activities help students take responsibility for their own learning.

Cross-Cultural Communication. Students compare different aspects of their own culture(s) with those of the English-speaking target culture.

Using the Text

Speaking Solutions is designed to be flexible. An abundance of material is provided to enable you to select activities that suit the particular needs of your class. You should definitely **not** feel obliged to cover every section, every activity, or every situation within an activity. With advanced students, you may work quickly through the first two units of the book, covering a limited number of activities, in order to spend more time on the later units. With intermediate students, however, you will probably work more carefully through the earlier units of the text in order to prepare students for the later units.

As much as possible, class time should be devoted to carrying out activities. While the information provided in the text is useful, it is not an efficient use of class time to read this material aloud. You can assign parts of the text as homework and then use class time to review and discuss the important points. As the course progresses, you may assign individual students to take charge of reviewing and discussing certain parts. Another way to maximize class interaction is to have students do all individual work as homework, not in class. For example, a number of activities involve students in filling out charts individually and then comparing answers in a group. By filling out their individual answers as homework, students can spend class time interacting and discussing their ideas. If class time is limited, here are some ways to move through the material more quickly:

- In activities that include several different situations, limit the number of situations that students discuss.
- If students need to listen to a listening passage several times, have them use a language lab (if available) for repeated listening sessions.
- Have students do the pronunciation activities in a language lab (if available).

Class Atmosphere

In a speaking/listening course, students' anxieties and inhibitions can interfere with their learning. For this reason, it is important to establish a friendly, relaxed classroom atmosphere. It may help students to think of the classroom as a laboratory where they can experiment and take risks with the language. In this atmosphere, students should realize that errors are a natural and expected part of learning a language.

Many of the activities in this text focus on real-life dilemmas and controversial issues. They are intended to generate polite disagreement and stimulate discussion of different points of view. It is important for students to understand that there are no right or wrong opinions or decisions. One of the goals of this text is to encourage students to examine their own opinions and values while at the same time showing respect for the opinions and values of others. With this in mind, it is important for the teacher to establish an atmosphere that is accepting of a diversity of student views.

Group Work

Many of the activities in this text involve the students in group work. Generally, groups composed of four members seem to work the best. Groups of three or five members may also be effective, depending on the activity. The first unit includes guidelines for organizing group work, with students taking on the following roles: leader, reader, summarizer, reporter, and observer (if necessary). Organizing all group activities in this way makes the course truly learner-centered since students must take full responsibility for carrying out each activity. As for seating, group members should arrange their seats or chairs in a small circle to encourage interaction.

Monitoring Activities

During pair or group activities, you should circulate (as unobtrusively as possible) from group to group. This helps ensure that students are on task and are using English. While you should not participate in pair or group activities, you need to stay involved in what the students are doing. Depending on the seating arrangement, you may want to sit in a desk or chair slightly behind the group.

One important reason to circulate during activities is to keep track of the kinds of problems students are having—grammatical accuracy, fluency, word choice, pronunciation/intonation, turntaking, discussion strategies, and so forth. Clearly, the most serious problems are those that interfere with communication. In any case, it is generally not effective to correct students' errors when they are involved in an activity. The most practical way to deal with communication problems is to make notes—discreetly—of what you observe as you are circulating. You can then use this information to provide feedback after the activity or to develop future lessons.

Evaluating Student Performance

At the beginning of the course, when they need to build up their confidence, students benefit most from encouragement and positive reinforcement. If at all possible, you should not evaluate or grade the students' first few efforts at speaking in a group or to the class. Many students suffer such anxiety in speaking situations that any criticism at this stage can be counterproductive.

After some practice, students can certainly benefit from constructive comments about their relative strengths and weaknesses, from both the teacher and peers. The evaluation forms in Appendix A, different for each unit, provide criteria for analyzing the effectiveness of group and individual communication. These evaluation forms may be used by the teacher and/or students to provide written feedback to speakers on their performance in group discussions and individual presentations.

Evaluating students does not necessarily mean grading them. Students often have enough anxiety about speaking without adding anxiety about grades. However, the unfortunate reality is that many programs require formal evaluations or grades. Even so, you should try to postpone assigning grades until later in the term. You can then use the rating scales on the evaluation forms to determine an overall grade for a discussion or presentation.

Course Components

The course consists of a student's book and an audiotape. In addition, an instructor's manual is available free of charge from the publisher. This manual provides detailed teaching suggestions and also contains the script of the audiotape.

Acknowledgments

In writing this book, I again realized how many people actually contribute to the development of a book attributed to one author. I would like to begin by expressing my sincere appreciation to Phil Edmondson, my colleague at George Washington University, for his extremely valuable contributions. I believe that his expertise and insight significantly improved the quality of the text.

I would also like to thank Stacy Capra for her special efforts: scrupulously reviewing the manuscript, helping select the photographs, participating in the recording of the pilot audiotape, brainstorming titles, providing ongoing encouragement, and navigating the New Jersey Turnpike on our trek to Englewood Cliffs.

I wish to express my further gratitude to the following people: Diane Pinkley, for reviewing/editing the manuscript, offering helpful suggestions, and always making me laugh; Eliza Reilly and Van Gosse, for participating in the recording of the original audiotape used in piloting the text; Mary Anne Saunders, Richard Tucker, and Robert Werckle, for their patience, good humor, and skill in recording the revised version of the audiotape; Belle Tyndall, for her support and encouragement; Anne Riddick, for helping me regain momentum in writing this book; Nancy Baxer of Prentice Hall Regents, for patiently answering all my questions and providing assistance throughout the project; Ellen Gratkowski of Prentice Hall Regents, for persevering in her search for appropriate photographs; and Peggy Gordon of P. M. Gordon Associates, for her valuable advice in the production of this book.

The Prentice Hall Regents reviewers deserve special mention for their many useful comments and suggestions: Suzanne M. Koons, Harvard University/MIT; Kevin McClure, ELS San Francisco; Paul Abraham, English Language Institute, Bradford College; Maida Kennedy-Xiao, Washington State University; Natalie Gast, Customized Language Skills Training; Sylvia D. Welyczko; and Mark Sawyer.

I would like to thank my colleagues who graciously allowed me into their classrooms with a camera and the students who bravely agreed to be photographed by a truly amateur photographer. I would also like to thank my students for their helpful feedback as I experimented with a wide variety of activities.

Finally, I would like to express my appreciation to my parents for their unfailing support and encouragement for as long as I can remember.

Unit 0

Getting Acquainted

At the beginning of this course, you may feel nervous about speaking English. However, you can feel more comfortable by getting to know the other members of your class.

Activity 1:   Making Introductions

1. In this activity, you will be interviewing a classmate and introducing him or her to the class. That person will then interview and introduce you. Before starting the interviews, however, work in a group or as a class to make a list of questions you can ask to get the following information about one another:

   A. Name, nickname
   B. Nationality: country and city of birth?
   C. Family information: married or single? children?
   D. Past Education: years? place? major? degrees?
   E. Current occupation

      • If a student: full- or part-time? major? graduate or undergraduate?
      • If a worker: full- or part-time? place? position? duties?

   F. English studies: years? place?
   G. Other languages spoken or studied
   H. Other places lived
   I. Travel
   J. Future plans
   K. Free time activities: hobbies? sports? other interests?
   L. Reasons for studying English or taking this course

2. Review the boxes "Appealing to the Speaker" and "Introducing Someone to a Group" following this activity. You may want to add other expressions to these lists.
3. Now work with a partner. If possible, choose someone you don't know, who speaks a different native language. Spend about fifteen minutes getting the information listed in item 1. You may take brief notes to help you remember important facts.
4. When you have finished interviewing each other, take a minute or two to review your notes.
5. Take turns introducing each other to the class. Remember to look at your audience as you are speaking. You may look at your notes, but do not read your introduction. Use details in your introduction to make your partner interesting to the other students.

APPEALING TO THE SPEAKER

In a conversation or discussion, you may not hear or understand what someone has said. In this case, you may need to make certain requests:

If You Need the Speaker to Repeat Something

> Pardon?
> Excuse me?
> Could you please repeat that?
> Would you mind repeating your question?

If the Speaker Is Talking Too Quickly

> I'm sorry. Could you please speak a little more slowly?
> Would you mind speaking more slowly? I couldn't quite follow what you said.

If the Speaker Is Talking Too Softly

> Sorry, I didn't hear what you said.
> Would you mind speaking a little louder?

If You Do Not Understand the Speaker

> I'm sorry, but I'm not sure I understand.
> Sorry, but I don't understand what you mean.
> I'm not sure I follow you. Did you say that . . . ?

If You Need More Help

> How do you $\left\{ \begin{array}{l} \text{pronounce} \\ \text{spell} \end{array} \right\}$ that?
>
> Would you please $\left\{ \begin{array}{l} \text{pronounce} \\ \text{spell} \end{array} \right\}$ that?

INTRODUCING SOMEONE TO A GROUP

To Begin

> Good morning. I'd like to introduce Mary Baker to you today.
> Today, I'd like to present John Smith to all of you.

To Close

I enjoyed talking to Mary Baker today, and I look forward to talking to her more in the future. Thank you.
After this introduction, I hope you all know John Smith a little better. Thank you.

Activity 2: Finding Similarities and Differences

1. Work in a small group. Spend ten minutes listing as many similarities and differences among you as you can. In what ways are you *all* alike? In what ways are you *all* different? You might think of such points as family size, habits, likes, dislikes, and opinions. Also consider topics such as favorite foods, music, movies, and actors.
2. Make a list of these similarities and differences.
3. When all the groups have finished, share your results as a class.

Activity 3: Interviewing Classmates

1. The purpose of this activity is to see who can find the most people in your class who fit the descriptions listed in item 4. You will have twelve minutes.
2. Speak to one person at a time. Speak *only* English!! Ask each person a specific question, such as, "Do you speak French?" The person will answer either "Yes, I do," or "No, I don't." Continue interviewing one person until you receive a "yes" answer. Write the person's name on the line beside the description. Then, move on to another person and repeat the process.
3. Remember that *you* must write the person's name on your list. The person does *not* write his or her own name.
4. Use a person's name only once.

   Find someone who . . .

   A. Has only one brother _____

   B. Speaks French _____

   C. Likes to cook _____

   D. Owns a car _____

   E. Dislikes cold weather _____

   F. Has a cat _____

   G. Plays the piano _____

   H. Likes to get up early in the morning _____

   I. Hates Coca-Cola _____

   J. Usually goes to bed before 11:00 _____

   K. Takes naps in the afternoons _____

   L. Jogs _____

   M. Seldom watches television _____

   N. Dislikes chocolate _____

   O. Often goes to the movies _____

   P. Regularly listens to the radio _____

   Q. Writes many letters _____

   R. Often eats pizza _____

   S. Makes many long-distance phone calls _____

   T. Plays soccer _____

  5. At the end of twelve minutes, discuss your findings as a class.

Activity 4:   Making a Recording to Introduce Yourself

  1. Work individually. If possible, do this activity at home or in the language laboratory outside of class. Since this activity involves making an audio recording, you will need a cassette tape recorder, a microphone (if necessary), and a blank audiotape.

  2. Think of information you might include in an audio recording to introduce yourself to the teacher. Look over the interview information in Activity 1 for some ideas. Make brief notes, if you wish, but do not write out sentences to read.

3. When you feel prepared, make a recording to introduce yourself to the teacher. Do the best you can, but do not worry if you make mistakes.
4. Write your name and date on the tape and give it to your teacher.

As the final step of the next two activities, a representative from each group is asked to report the group's results to the class. It is important for all group members to help the representative prepare a brief, well-organized report to present to the class. The representative may use notes while presenting the information, but should not read the report. The following box includes some guidelines and sample expressions that might be useful in preparing such a group report.

REPORTING YOUR GROUP'S RESULTS TO THE CLASS

Here are some sample expressions you can use to report the results of Activity 5 to the class. You can use similar expressions in reporting the results of other activities in this text.

Beginning Your Report

Mention the names of the group members and the purpose of the discussion.

> Mary, John, Frank, Anne, and I had an interesting discussion on the activities we feel are the most important for us to learn in this course.

Summarizing Your Results

> During our discussion, we decided that . . . .
> To summarize our discussion, we agreed that . . . .

All of us	think . . . .
Most of us	believe . . . .
Many of us	feel . . . .
	prefer . . . .
	want . . . .

Some of us thought . . . while others thought . . . .

Organizing Your Main Points

Notice how the main points are organized by using the words *first*, *then*, and *finally*.

> To sum up our discussion, we *first* agreed on three activities that we think are very important for us to learn: participating in class discussions; making presentations; and speaking informally to a small group. Most of us also think that participating in business meetings is very important. *Then*, most of us felt that two activities are important, but not very important: dealing informally with people at work and leading discussions. *Finally*, we all agreed on two activities that we think are not important for us to learn: watching television and presenting papers at conferences.

Concluding Your Report

> I believe that this summarizes our results. Do you have any questions?

Activity 5: Considering Your Needs

1. Work individually. Consider the following list of activities in which you need or will need to use English. Which do you feel are the most important for you to learn in this course? Using the following key, write your answers in the column labeled *You*. For now, leave the other columns blank.

    + = very important   √ = important   − = not important

SPEAKING AND LISTENING ACTIVITIES IN ENGLISH	YOU				
A. Dealing with people in social situations					
B. Participating in class discussions or seminars					
C. Participating in business meetings					
D. Leading discussions or meetings					
E. Speaking informally to a small group					
F. Making presentations or giving reports					
G. Taking academic courses					
H. Dealing informally with people at school or work					
I. Presenting papers at meetings or conferences					
J. Understanding television programs and films					
K. Other:					

2. Work in a small group of three or four people. Write each person's name at the top of a column in the chart. Exchange information so you can fill in the chart.
3. Work together to discuss the following:

   - Which activities are *very important* for members of your group?
   - Which activities are *important* for members of your group?
   - Which activities are *not important* for members of your group?

4. When all the groups have finished, a representative from each group should report the group's results to the class.

Activity 6:   Considering Outside Resources

1. Work individually. How many of the following resources—*in English*—are available to you at school, at work, or in your community? Put a check in the column labeled *Are Available* to show the ones that are available. In the other column, labeled *You Have Used*, use the following key to indicate how often you have used each resource:

   + = frequently   √ = sometimes   − = never

RESOURCES IN ENGLISH	ARE AVAILABLE	YOU HAVE USED
A. Television programs		
B. Movies		
C. Videos		
D. Radio programs		
E. Books and/or magazines		
F. Newspapers		
G. Language lab and/or media resources center		
H. Computer programs		
I. Music records, cassettes, and compact discs		
J. English-language clubs		
K. English-speaking people		
L. Other:		

2. Work in a small group. Discuss the following:

- Which resources are available in your area?
- Which resources have people in your group tried?
- Which resources have members of your group found to be the most useful?
- Which resources do people in your group plan to try (or to use again) in the near future?

3. When all the groups have finished, a representative from each group should report the group's results to the class.

Unit 1
Interacting in Class

LISTENING TO A LECTURE

WORKING WITH A PARTNER

WORKING IN A GROUP

GIVING A PRESENTATION

- How do you think the students feel in each situation shown above?
- What are the advantages and disadvantages of each type of activity?
- What kinds of activities in English class do you enjoy the most?
- What kinds of activities do you enjoy the least?

Listening Practice

Activity 1:   Identifying Expressions

1. Listen to Activity 1 on the tape. You will hear eight dialogues about getting acquainted. In each dialogue, the second speaker is having some problem understanding the first speaker. What does the second speaker ask or say in order to deal with the problem? Write each question or statement in the blank.

   A. _____

   B. _____

   C. _____

   D. _____

   E. _____

   F. _____

   G. _____

   H. _____

2. Work in a small group or as a class to compare your answers.

Activity 2:   Identifying Relationships

1. Listen to Activity 2 on the tape. You will hear ten dialogues. For each dialogue, identify the relationship between the speakers. Using the following key, write the appropriate number in each blank:

   1 = employer-employee
   2 = teacher-student
   3 = classmates
   4 = co-workers
   5 = strangers

   A. _____   C. _____

   B. _____   D. _____

E. _____   H. _____

F. _____   I. _____

G. _____   J. _____

2. Work in a small group or as a class to compare your answers.

Communication Skills

Organizing Small Group Activities

During this course, you will be participating in many small group activities. You can make sure that every member takes an active part in a group activity by giving each person a role: leader, reader, summarizer, reporter, or observer. The following instructions explain how to organize a small group discussion with four or five members:

Group members sit in a circle. One student takes (or is assigned) Role 1. Students then count off in order—2, 3, 4, 5—so that #2 takes Role 2, #3 takes Role 3, and so forth. In this way, each group member has a specific role to play in the activity. If an activity has more than one situation, group mem-

bers rotate roles after each situation. This gives everyone a chance to take on a different role during the activity.

Here is a list of the different roles with a brief explanation of the responsibilities of each:

Role 1: *Leader*

- Starts the activity
- Makes sure everyone participates
- Keeps everyone on the subject
- Keeps the discussion moving
- Keeps track of the time

Role 2: *Reader*

- Reads aloud the instructions, situation(s), questions, etc.

Role 3: *Summarizer*

- Explains the situation or problem in his or her own words (without reading)
- Makes sure everyone understands the situation

Role 4: *Reporter*

- Reports the group's results or ideas to the class

Role 5: *Observer [when necessary]*

- Observes the group or an individual
- Fills out observation forms

During each activity, all group members should participate actively. Each person:

- Presents ideas
- Supports ideas with examples, details, and reasons
- Asks other for their ideas

Finally, all group members (not only the reporter) should fill in the blanks in each activity as a record of their group's ideas and decisions.

Activity 3:   Organizing a Small Group Discussion

1. Work in a small group of four or five people. Follow the instructions presented in the previous section for organizing small group activities. Group members should take the roles of leader, reader, summarizer, and reporter. No observer is needed in this activity.
2. As a group, consider the following situation and discussion question:

   Situation. An old, homeless man spends every day in the public library. For most of the day, he sits quietly reading newspapers, magazines, and books. Many people in the library have complained that the man is extremely dirty and smells terrible. Also, they say that he sometimes stares at them in a strange way that makes them nervous. The homeless man, however, says that he does nothing to bother anybody.

   Discussion. What are possible ways that library officials might deal with this situation?

   A. _____

   B. _____

   C. _____

   D. _____

   E. _____

3. Work as a class. On the blackboard, list all the different ideas developed by the groups.
4. Get back into your original small group. Work together to reach agreement on the following question:

   Group Decision. What is the best way for library officials to deal with this situation?

   _____

   _____

5. When your group has reached a decision, discuss the following:

   - Did each group member take his or her role during the discussion? If not, why not?
   - Did all group members take an active part in reaching the final decision? If not, why not?
   - How can you improve your next discussion?

6. When all the groups have finished, work as a class to compare the decision each group reached. Which decision seems to be the best? To conclude this activity, compare your answers to the questions in item 5.

Brainstorming

An important technique that you will be using in this course is called *brainstorming*. The purpose of brainstorming is to produce as many ideas as possible on a particular topic. Then you can later select the *best* ideas to use in a discussion or a presentation. You can brainstorm individually, in pairs, or in groups. Here are some general guidelines for group brainstorming:

* Write the topic at the top of a sheet of paper.
* Say anything on the topic that comes to mind, even if it seems silly, wild, or crazy.
* Do not discuss or judge any idea that is mentioned. List all ideas without comment.
* Write quickly, using words or short phrases. Do not worry about grammar or spelling.
* Get everyone in the group involved. Keep the ideas flowing!
* Try to build on or add to ideas suggested by others.
* Remember that quantity is more important than quality.

At the end of the time period, review the ideas you have developed. At this point you may want to:

* Cross out any ideas that do not seem to fit.
* Put a check next to the most useful or interesting ideas.
* Spend a few more minutes adding any new ideas that come to mind.

The most important "rule" of brainstorming is not to judge the ideas as they are mentioned. People need to relax in order to be able to think of interesting, creative ideas. Try the following activity to get an idea of how group brainstorming works.

Activity 4:   Practicing Group Brainstorming

1. Work in a small group to consider the following:

   Situation. David Doolittle is an unusual student. He always goes to class, but he never does his homework. He is intelligent and imaginative, so he always has a different excuse to explain why he did not do his homework. Today, however, he is having trouble thinking of an excuse.

2. Spend ten minutes brainstorming excuses that David can give his teacher. For example, "A robber broke into my house last night and stole it." "My dog ate it for breakfast." Use your imagination and have fun thinking of ideas. Try to produce a list of at least twenty excuses.

3. When all the groups have finished, work as a class to share the ideas of each group. Then discuss the following:

   - How many ideas did each group develop?
   - Did each group follow all the brainstorming "rules"?
   - In general, how comfortable did everyone feel using this technique?
   - How do you think you can improve future brainstorming sessions?

Sometimes group members do not participate equally in a brainstorming session. One way to give everyone a chance is to use "chain" brainstorming. In a "chain," group members sit in a circle facing each other. You then go around the circle, giving each group member a turn to offer an idea. If a person does not have an idea, he or she can say "Pass," and the next person takes a turn. During a brainstorming session, you should always keep in mind that quantity is more important than quality. Therefore, *any* idea is better than *no* idea.

Activity 5:   Practicing Chain Brainstorming

1. Work in a small group. Think about students who are good or successful language learners. What do you think makes them good learners?
2. Spend ten minutes chain brainstorming possible ideas. The reporter should write every idea as it is mentioned.
3. At the end of ten minutes, review your ideas.

   - Cross out any ideas that do not seem to fit.
   - Spend one or two more minutes adding any new ideas that come to mind.

4. When you have finished, discuss the following:

   - Did you follow the rules for chain brainstorming? If not, why not?
   - Did you feel more comfortable brainstorming this time? Why or why not?
   - What are the advantages and disadvantages of chain brainstorming?
   - How do you think you can improve future brainstorming sessions?

5. When all the groups have finished, discuss the following as a class:

   - How many ideas did each group develop?
   - In what situations do you think brainstorming might be useful?

Using Appropriate Language Styles

In English, as in most languages, speakers use different levels of formality:

Formal/Indirect

- I'm very sorry, but I'm afraid I didn't quite understand your last point. I would appreciate it if you could explain it again.
- Would you be so kind as to repeat your last point?

Neutral/Polite

- Would you mind explaining your last point, please?
- Could you please explain that again?

Informal/direct

- Excuse me?
- Can you explain that?
- Please explain that.

Highly Informal

- What are you talking about?
- What?
- Huh?

Generally, speakers of English use more formal language with people in authority or of much higher status. People speaking in a formal situation tend to use correct grammar and speak in complete sentences. Furthermore, they usually speak more carefully, more clearly, and more slowly. On the other hand, people use informal language with friends and family. When speaking informally, they may use a more "relaxed" pronunciation, such as "I'm gonna leave" ["I'm going to leave."] or "They wanna leave" ["They want to leave."]. In an informal situation, people may also speak more quickly, omit words, and use slang.

Of course, language is not neatly divided into formal and informal styles. There are various levels of formality between the two. In fact, you will find that a neutral/polite style of language—between formal and informal—is generally appropriate in most academic and professional situations. As a learner of English, you may find that it is safer to sound slightly more formal than to be too informal. Of course, as you become friends with your co-workers or classmates, you will probably move toward a more informal style of language. Keep in mind, though, that an informal style may sound rude or disrespectful in a business situation. For this reason, all of the language presented in this book is neutral/polite in style. As you get to know people better and improve your speaking ability, you will feel more comfortable changing your speaking style to suit the situation, the subject, and the people involved.

In general, in choosing the appropriate level of formality, you need to consider the following:

- What is your *relationship* to the other speaker? Are you relatives, friends, acquaintances, or strangers?
- What is the other speaker's *professional role*? Is he or she your co-worker, your boss, or a high-level official?

- What is the *setting*? Are you at a job interview, a business meeting, a staff picnic, or a party?
- What *subject* are you discussing? Are you dealing with typical work-related matters, asking for a favor, or making a serious complaint?

Of course, most speaking situations involve some or all of these factors, not just one. Your choice of language style, then, will depend on a combination of these factors.

Activity 6: Identifying Appropriate Language Styles

1. Work with a partner. For each of the following situations, write *F* (formal) or *I* (informal) to show whether you might switch your language style slightly to one or the other style; write *N* (neutral) if you think a neutral style would be appropriate.

———— **A.** Asking your boss for a raise

———— **B.** Discussing a homework assignment with a classmate

———— **C.** Asking a friend to go out for a cup of coffee

———— **D.** Being interviewed for a job

———— **E.** Asking the teacher about a homework assignment

———— **F.** Asking the teacher to raise your grade on an important writing assignment

———— **G.** Having a meeting at work with several co-workers

———— **H.** Presenting a paper at a scientific conference

———— **I.** Talking with an important government leader at an official reception

———— **J.** Complaining to a co-worker about a serious mistake he made

———— **K.** Asking a classmate to spend an hour or two helping you with some work you missed

2. When all the pairs have finished, compare your ideas as a class.

Participating in Class

The way that students and teachers interact varies from culture to culture. As a result, the way students act in one culture may seem strange or even rude in another culture.

The following guidelines are generally appropriate in the United States or in a class with an American teacher. Of course, even within the United States, student-teacher interaction varies from class to class and from teacher to teacher. Therefore, be sure to discuss the following guidelines with your teacher. Are they different from the ones you have followed in other classes?

1. Find out what your teacher prefers to be called. In some classes, teachers and students call each other by their first names. In other classes, teachers want students to call them by their last names with a title, such as Dr. White, Professor Green, Mr. Brown, or Ms. Black. Generally, though, students do not call the teacher, "Teacher."

2. Take initiative in class. Show your interest by volunteering to answer questions. Ask questions when you do not understand something or when you need more information. In general, teachers expect students to take an active part in class. Many teachers include class participation as part of the final course grade. Furthermore, teachers may have an unfavorable impression of students who never make comments or ask questions. They may feel that these students are not paying attention, are not prepared, or are not interested.

3. Respond immediately if the teacher calls on you to answer a question. Whether or not you know the answer, make eye contact with the teacher and say something. (This unit includes expressions you can use if you need a few moments to think or if you don't know the answer.) Teachers expect a direct response to a question, and it may seem rude if you do not say anything. Furthermore, if you remain silent, even for a few seconds, the teacher may call on another student or someone else may jump in to answer the question.

SPEAKING OUT IN CLASS

Signaling You Want to Speak

To get the teacher's attention, you can simply raise your hand. You may also call the teacher by name. Sometimes you can signal that you want to speak by leaning forward and making eye contact with the teacher. If the teacher doesn't notice these signals, you can also say:

> Excuse me, ...
> May I ask a question?
> Could I make a comment?

Holding the Floor

When the teacher calls on you, you can give yourself a moment or two to think before answering by:

- Hesitating
  Well, umm . . . .
  Umm, let's see.
  Umm, let me see.
  Let me think.

- Repeating or rephrasing the question
  In other words, you want to know . . . .
  So, you're asking me . . . .

- Asking the instructor to repeat the question if you didn't understand
  Would you mind repeating the question, please?
  Would you please repeat that?

Avoiding Answering

> I'm not really sure.
> I don't really know.
> I'm afraid I don't know.
> I'm sorry, but I don't know.

Activity 7:   Volunteering in Class

1. Work as a class. Students should take turns acting as the "teacher," while the others close their books. The "teacher" asks one of the following questions and then waits for the students to volunteer answers. Students should give examples, details, and/or reasons to explain their answers. The purpose is for everyone to participate as much as possible—without

waiting to be called on by the "teacher." However, the "teacher" may also call on students to answer. After several answers, the "teacher" can go on to another question. There are no right or wrong answers to these questions, so relax and have fun.

A. Of all the things you do in your free time, what do you enjoy the most?
B. What is the best present you have ever received?
C. What do you think is the perfect age to be?
D. What is your favorite holiday?
E. Which would you rather be—the youngest or the oldest child in the family?
F. If you could spend the day with one famous person alive in the world today, whom would you choose?
G. Which pet do you think is better—a dog or a cat?
H. What place in the world would you most like to visit?
I. What was your favorite subject in high school?
J. What do you like best about the city where you are living?
K. What do you *not* like about the city where you are living?
L. What's your favorite place to be alone?
M. Think about the worst teacher you ever had. What made that teacher so terrible?

2. As you participate in this activity, use a separate sheet of paper to put a check each time you volunteer to speak. (Do not count the times the "teacher" calls on you.) Remember—keep your book closed during this activity! You have to listen to the questions.
3. The teacher or observers may use the Class Participation Evaluation Form in Appendix A.
4. When you have finished, discuss this activity as a class:

- Did you find it easy or difficult to volunteer your answers?
- How many times did each person volunteer?
- Did everyone in class participate actively? If not, what happened?

Pronunciation Practice

Word Stress

To understand word stress, you need to know what a *syllable* is. A syllable is the part of a word that contains one vowel sound along with one or more consonant sounds. In general, the number of vowel sounds in a word determines the number of syllables. Another way to understand this is to think of syllables as the number of beats in a word.

Activity 8:   Counting Syllables

Listen to Activity 8 on the tape. As you listen to the following words, tap your finger or pencil on the desk to help you count the number of syllables.

1 Syllable	2 Syllables	3 Syllables	4 Syllables
part	number	following	dictionary
word	useful	determines	repetition
group	pencil	expression	understanding
sound	pronounce	correctly	presentation
think	contain	consonant	experience

Activity 9:   Counting Syllables

Listen to Activity 9 on the tape. Repeat each word after the speaker. Write the number of syllables that you hear.

1. _____	5. _____	9. _____	13. _____
2. _____	6. _____	10. _____	14. _____
3. _____	7. _____	11. _____	15. _____
4. _____	8. _____	12. _____	16. _____

In English, words of more than one syllable have a stress, or accent, on one of the syllables. Stressing the right syllable is an important part of the correct pronunciation. If you stress the wrong part of the word, people may not understand you. You put stress on a particular syllable by:

- Holding it longer
- Saying it at a higher pitch
- Pronouncing the vowel sound clearly

Thus, the stressed (or accented) syllable may sound longer, higher, and stronger than the other syllables in the word. Each word, then, has one stressed syllable while the others are unstressed or weak syllables. There is a greater difference between stressed and unstressed syllables in English than in most other languages. This is because English speakers tend to give careful pronunciation to the stressed syllable, and then "reduce" (or weaken) the other unstressed syllables. By reduce, we mean that people usually pronounce unstressed syllables in a relaxed way—either /*uh*/ (as in *up*) or /*ih*/ (as in *it*).

Some words in English can be used as either nouns or verbs. The difference in stress indicates the difference in usage: the noun has the stress on the first syllable, while the verb has the stress on the second syllable.

Activity 10: Focusing on Word Stress

Listen to Activity 10 on the tape. In each item you will first hear the noun and then the verb. Notice that the stressed syllables are written in capital letters in the following list. Pay close attention to the way that stress affects the pronunciation of each word. Repeat each word after the speaker, being careful to stress the right syllable.

	Nouns	**Verbs**
1.	CON duct	con DUCT
2.	CON trast	con TRAST
3.	DE crease	de CREASE
4.	IN crease	in CREASE
5.	IN sult	in SULT
6.	OB ject	ob JECT
7.	PER mit	per MIT
8.	PRES ent	pre SENT
9.	PROG ress	pro GRESS
10.	PRO duce	pro DUCE
11.	REC ord	re CORD
12.	SUB ject	sub JECT

Activity 11: Identifying Stressed Syllables

Listen to Activity 11 on the tape. The speaker will say each word twice. Repeat each word after the speaker. Circle the syllable that is stressed.

1. pre sent
2. re cord
3. con trast
4. con duct
5. in crease
6. ob ject

7. prog ress
8. in sult
9. sub ject
10. prod uce
11. per mit
12. de crease

Activity 12: Identifying Stressed Syllables

Listen to Activity 12 on the tape. The speaker will say each word twice. Repeat each word after the speaker. Circle the syllable that is stressed.

1. at ten tion
2. ex am ple
3. un der stand
4. dif fi cult
5. in tro duce
6. nec es sar y
7. mis take
8. re la tion ship
9. com pre hen sion
10. sit u a tion

11. op por tu ni ty
12. ac a dem ic
13. dis cus sion
14. ques tion
15. ap pro pri ate
16. pro nun ci a tion
17. au di ence
18. par tic i pate
19. pro fes sion al
20. con fi dent

Learning Strategies

Analyzing Needs

Speaking a foreign language requires several different skills. By identifying your problem areas, you will know which skills to focus on in this course.

Activity 13: Identifying Skill Areas for Improvement

1. Work individually. As you begin this course, think about the areas in your speaking and listening ability that you feel need the most improvement. In the column labeled *You*, write *1* for the area you feel needs the most work, *2* for the next, etc. For now, leave the other columns blank.

SKILL AREAS	YOU			
A. Grammar				
B. Vocabulary				
C. Pronunciation				
D. Fluency: speaking smoothly, without hesitating or repeating too much				
E. Listening comprehension: understanding what others say				
F. Feeling confident about speaking				
G. Other:				

2. Now work in a small group with two or three other people. Write each person's name at the top of a column in the chart. Exchange information so you can fill in the chart.
3. As a group, discuss the skills that members of your group feel they need to work on the most.
4. When all the groups have finished, share your results as a class.

Activity 14: Considering Strategies for Improvement

1. Work in a small group. Think about your experiences in learning English. In what ways have you tried to improve each skill area? For example, how do you study a new grammatical structure, such as a verb tense? Do you go over the rule until you memorize it? Do you try to find examples of this structure in your reading? Do you try to practice it while speaking?

2. As a group, brainstorm a list of strategies that people can use to improve their skills in English. Be as specific as possible. Each group member should record these ideas on a separate sheet of paper. Be sure to consider all of the skill areas listed in the chart in Activity 13.
3. After your group has finished brainstorming, discuss the strategies that seem the best, the most interesting, and the most unusual. Which new strategies might group members try?
4. When all the groups have finished, share your ideas as a class.

Cross-Cultural Communication

Considering Classroom Behavior

Classroom behavior varies from culture to culture. Behavior that is acceptable in one culture may seem rude in another culture. In many cases, appropriate behavior depends on the circumstances of the particular situation. The following expressions may be useful as you work on Activity 15.

EXPLAINING SPECIAL CIRCUMSTANCES

It depends on {
how old you are.
who the other person is.
what you are talking about.
where you are.
}

If {
you know the teacher,
it is a university class,
you are in high school,
you are in a large class,
} then you {
should . . . . .
can . . . . .
}

Activity 15:   Considering Appropriate Behavior

1. Work individually on the following questionnaire. Write what you know about your own culture and what you think is usual in American culture. Do not limit yourself to the given examples. Feel free to use your own ideas.

IN YOUR CULTURE	SITUATIONS	IN AMERICAN CULTURE
	A. When the teacher walks in and says, "Good morning," what do you do? • Stand up and say, "Good morning." • Stay seated, look at the teacher, and say, "Good morning." • Look down and remain silent. • Smile but say nothing.	
	B. Class begins at 10:00, but you arrive at 10:15. The door is closed, but you hear the teacher talking to the class. What do you do? • Walk in, say hello to the other students, and take your seat. • Knock on the door to ask the teacher whether you can come in. • Decide not to go to class, and later explain to the teacher. • Walk in quietly, sit down in the nearest seat, and explain to the teacher after class. • Wait outside the door until there is a break or class is over.	

IN YOUR CULTURE	SITUATIONS	IN AMERICAN CULTURE
	C. Which of the following habits are not acceptable in class? • Chewing gum • Resting with your head down on the desk • Sleeping • Sitting with one or both shoes off • Sitting with a foot or leg up on a chair or seat • Eating a sandwich or a candy bar • Drinking a soft drink • Doing homework for another class • Talking with another student while the teacher is speaking	

2. When everyone has finished, share your answers as a class.
3. Turn to the Answer Key on page 221 to see some typical responses of people in the United States.

Unit 2

Maintaining a Conversation

TALKING WITH A STRANGER

TALKING WITH FRIENDS

TALKING WITH A CO-WORKER

TALKING WITH YOUR BOSS

In your country, which of the following topics do you usually talk about in each situation? Which do you *not* talk about?

- Movies
- Family problems
- Food/restaurants
- Recent trips or vacations
- Sports
- Problems with your boss
- Health problems

- Books
- Television programs
- Classes/teachers
- Current events
- Politics
- Religion
- Free-time activities

Listening Practice

Activity 1:   Identifying Expressions

1. Review the box "Encouraging Conversation" in this unit.
2. Now listen to Activity 1 on the tape. In each of the eight brief conversational exchanges, the second speaker responds with a brief comment or question and then asks an information question to keep the conversation going. As you listen, write the brief comment or question that the second speaker uses to respond to the first speaker.

BRIEF COMMENTS OR QUESTIONS	INFORMATION QUESTIONS
A.	
B.	
C.	
D.	
E.	
F.	
G.	
H.	

3. Listen to the tape again. This time, write the information question that the second speaker asks.
4. Work in a small group or as a class to compare your answers.

Activity 2:   Opening a Conversation

1. Listen to Activity 2 on the tape. For each of the six conversational exchanges, write the sentence or question that the first speaker uses to open the conversation.

A. _____

B. _____

C. _____

D. _____

E. _____

F. _____

2. Work in a small group or as a class to compare your answers.

Activity 3:   Closing a Conversation

1. Review the box "Closing a Conversation" in this unit. Then listen to Activity 3 on the tape. For each of the four conversations, write the expression that one of the speakers uses to signal the end of the conversation.

A. _____

B. _____

C. _____

D. _____

2. Work in a small group or as a class to compare your answers.

Communication Skills

Asking Questions

The ability to ask questions is an important skill in conversations and discussions. Questions are useful both in getting information and in involving others in a conversation. To use questions more effectively, you may find it helpful to understand the difference between closed and open questions.

Closed questions are those that can be answered with *yes*, *no*, or a one- or two-word response. For example, you might ask someone a closed question such as, "Do you like living in this city?" or "How long have you lived here?" Closed questions ask for specific information, so they limit the possible answers.

Open questions, on the other hand, encourage the other person to give more information. For instance, you might ask someone, "Why do you enjoy living in this city?," "How do you feel about attending this university?," or "What do you think about . . . ?" Open questions help to involve the other speaker actively in the conversation.

Activity 4:   Identifying Open and Closed Questions

1. Work with a partner or in a small group. The following are questions that an American might ask an international student at a university in the United States. Identify each as *O* (open) or *C* (closed).

_____ **A.** Where are you from?

_____ **B.** Why did you choose this university?

_____ **C.** How do universities in the United States compare with universities in your country?

_____ **D.** How long do you plan to stay here?

_____ **E.** What has surprised you most about life in this country?

_____ **F.** When did you arrive here?

_____ **G.** How do you like living in this city?

_____ **H.** How do you get to school?

_____ **I.** What do you think about the traffic here?

_____ **J.** Are you here with your family?

2. When all the groups have finished, compare your answers as a class.

Activity 5:   Asking Questions

1. Work with a partner. Consider the following statement: "I had a great vacation!" Make a list of twelve to fifteen questions you might ask to get more information. Think about the many question words that you can use: *who, what, what kind of, which, where, when, why, how, how long, how often, how many, how much,* etc.
2. After all the groups have finished, write some of these questions on the board or present them orally. Imagine asking a co-worker or classmate these questions. As a class, analyze each question:

   • Is it grammatically correct? If not, correct it.
   • Is it appropriate to ask this question? If not, why not?
   • Is it an open or closed question?

Activity 6:   Asking More Questions

1. Work individually. Spend one or two minutes thinking about a recent time that you:

   • Had a problem at work or school
   • Took a trip
   • Went to a restaurant, concert, or sports event
   • Did something on the weekend or in your free time
   • Worked on a hobby
   • Had a funny, strange, or terrible experience

2. Now work with a partner. Begin by commenting on one of these topics. Your partner should ask questions for three minutes to get as much information as possible.
3. Exchange roles so that your partner makes the opening comment. Again, the questioner should try to keep getting information for three minutes.
4. If time permits, change pairs to continue practicing.

Encouraging Communication

In a conversation, both speakers need to take responsibility for keeping the communication going. Of course, asking information questions is one way to do this. However, a conversation is not a question-and-answer session. You can also use several other strategies to encourage conversation. Consider the differences between the following two conversations:

Conversation 1

A: What do you do?
B: I'm an engineer.
A: What company do you work for?
B: IBM.
A: How long have you worked there?
B: Two years.
A: Do you like your job?
B: Yes, I do.

Conversation 2

A: What do you do?
B: I'm an engineer. How about you?
A: I'm a student.
B: Oh, really?
A: Yes, I'm studying business administration at State University.
B: I see. That sounds interesting.
A: Yes, it is. The program is hard, but I think I'm learning a lot. So, where do you work?
B: At IBM in New York City.
A: New York City? Do you like it there?

As Conversation 2 shows, you can use a number of strategies to encourage conversation. You can also use body language, such as looking at the speaker, smiling, or nodding, to show that you are listening.

ENCOURAGING CONVERSATION

Using a Short Response to Show That You Are Listening

I see.	Oh?
Of course.	Yes.
Really?	Mmmm.

Using an Auxiliary to Make a Question

A: The meeting started half an hour late!
B: It did?

A: I didn't take notes in last week's lecture.
B: Didn't you?

Do you? (You do?)	Don't you? (You don't?)
Were you? (You were?)	Weren't you? (You weren't?)
Have you? (You have?)	Can you? (You can?)

Repeating a Key Word or Phrase

A: I'm going to Paris next week.
B: Paris?

A: The meeting lasted for two hours.
B: Two hours?

Asking a Follow-up Information Question

What happened?
How was it?
What did you do then?

Activity 7:   Encouraging Communication

1. Work with a partner to develop an appropriate response to each of the following comments. This response should consist of a brief comment or question followed by a specific information question. Use some of the different types of responses listed in the box "Encouraging Conversation."

   A. I was almost late to work this morning.

   _____

   B. I'm thinking about going to Australia during my summer vacation.

   _____

   C. That meeting this morning really lasted a long time.

   _____

   D. This photocopier has broken down twice this week!

   _____

   E. I spent most of the weekend watching basketball on television.

   _____

   F. I saw a terrible accident this morning.

   _____

G. I met the new manager this morning.

_____

H. Yesterday was an incredibly busy day!

_____

2. When all the pairs have finished, compare your responses as a class.

Another way to keep a conversation going is to expand your comments, even if you can answer a question with just a word or two. In this case, you can add more specific information or details to your response. Consider the following exchanges:

Question: Do you like living in Washington, D.C.?

Short   Yes.
answers: Yes, I do.

Expanded   Yes, it's a beautiful city and there's always
answers: something interesting to do.
                Yes, but sometimes the traffic and noise can be terrible.

Activity 8:   Giving Expanded Answers

1. Work with a partner to develop expanded answers to each of the following closed questions:

A. Do you like living in this city?

_____

B. Are you a full-time student?

_____

C. Do you like to travel?

_____

D. Do you play any sports?

_____

E. Do you own a car?

_____

F. Do you like to watch TV?

_____

G. Did you do the homework last night?

_____

H. Have you ever been to Tahiti?

_____

2. When all the pairs have finished, compare your responses as a class.
3. With your partner, write four or five similar questions.
4. Now switch partners, and practice asking and answering the questions you developed.

Making Small Talk

One useful conversation skill is the ability to make _small talk,_ or casual, light discussion of everyday topics. This section focuses on small talk in academic and professional situations. In these cases, your goal is to maintain friendly relations with people you deal with. Small talk is especially important at work or school because it helps establish a friendly atmosphere and keeps relations smooth. Furthermore, in business situations, small talk helps make people feel more comfortable with each other before they move on to more serious matters.

The following information discusses how typical Americans handle small talk. You may have studied these conversation strategies in previous courses. If so, you can review them briefly before doing the activities. In any case, as you read or review this information, keep in mind that people from different cultures have different ways of handling conversations. You may want to consider these differences as you work through this section.

Finding Topics to Discuss

Small talk generally does not involve the speakers in personal details. With Americans, you should avoid topics that many people regard as too personal, such as age, weight, politics, personal money matters, sex, and religion. Some typical subjects for small talk include:

- Weather
- Work
- School
- Recent activities or experiences
- Future plans
- Sports

- Television programs
- Movies
- Vacation and travel plans
- Hobbies
- Free-time activities
- Current events

Activity 9:   Identifying Appropriate Topics

1. Work with a partner. Imagine that you are making small talk with an American you have just met. Which of the following questions would be inappropriate or too personal? Write *No* in front of those that you should *not* ask. Write *Yes* in front of those that would be appropriate.

_____ **A.** How old are you?

_____ **B.** What do you do?

_____ **C.** How much rent do you pay?

_____ **D.** Why aren't you married?

_____ **E.** What's your job like?

_____ **F.** Have you gained a little weight recently?

_____ **G.** What company do you work for?

_____ **H.** What's your major?

_____ **I.** You've been married for two years. Why don't you have any children?

_____ **J.** How many people are there in your family?

_____ **K.** Where did you go to university?

_____ **L.** How much money do you make?

_____ **M.** Where do you live?

_____ **N.** Where did you buy your books for this class?

_____ **O.** You're wearing a beautiful watch. How much did it cost?

2. Compare your answers as a class.
3. Work individually or with a partner. Make a list of questions that people should not ask in your culture. Share these questions with the class.

Exchanging Greetings

At school or work, you may regularly see people that you know only slightly. In these situations, Americans often simply nod and smile in a friendly way. They may also exchange brief greetings without stopping for longer conversations. The following is a typical exchange:

A: Hello. How are you doing?
B: Fine, thanks. How about you?

Greeting People You Know

Of course, there are many ways to greet people you know. Here is one example:

A: Hello, Jane. How are you?
B: Hello, Bob. I'm fine, thanks. I haven't seen you in a long time. How have you been?
A: I've been busy, but my vacation starts next week.

Introducing Yourself

In an academic or work situation, you may find yourself talking to someone whose name you want or need to know. If you don't know or can't remember that person's name, you can say:

A: Hello. I'm Carol Miller. I'm sorry, but I don't know your name.
B: I'm Jack Robbins. How are you?

A: Good morning. I know we've talked before, but I'm afraid I can't remember your name.
B: Yes, my name is Nancy Smith. And your name is . . . ?
A: George Nichols.
B: It's nice to meet you, Mr. Nichols.

Opening a Conversation

Generally, it isn't too difficult to open a conversation with people you know well. After greeting them, you can talk about your classes, homework, work, people you know, recent activities, etc. In other situations, however, you may find yourself sitting or standing next to someone you know only slightly. This often occurs when you are waiting for something—for class to start, for the elevator to arrive, for a meeting to begin, and so forth. In these situations, it might seem rude not to speak to the other person. Americans often open these types of conversations by talking about the weather or their surroundings:

A: It looks like it's going to rain, doesn't it?
B: Yes, it really looks terrible outside.

A: Isn't the weather great today?
B: Yes, it's a good day to be outside.

A: How long have you been waiting here?
B: About ten minutes. The meeting should begin soon.

A: Do you know many people here?
B: No, I don't. How about you?

Sometimes, the conversation may last a little longer if you know the other person better or if you have more time to talk.

Activity 10:   Opening a Conversation

1. Work with a partner. Imagine that you are acquaintances in each of the following situations. For each, develop a brief conversational exchange that includes:

    • Appropriate greetings
    • A comment or question to open the conversation
    • An appropriate response

    A. It's a rainy day. You arrive at the bus stop, where a co-worker is waiting for the bus.

B. You have a meeting at work with people from other departments. You walk into the conference room a little early. One participant is already in the room, waiting for the meeting to begin.

C. You are standing next to a colleague in the office. You are both waiting to use the photocopier, but several people are ahead of you.

D. You are waiting in line at the company cafeteria. When you look around, you notice that a new employee from your department is standing behind you.

2. When all the pairs have finished, take turns presenting some of your conversations to the class.

3. Work as a class. Develop openings for other situations in which you need to make small talk.

Closing a Conversation

In many situations, your conversation will end naturally—when the teacher arrives, when the meeting begins, or when the elevator arrives. These types of conversations can end very simply by one of the speakers saying:

Oh, here's the teacher.

It looks like the meeting is beginning.

Finally—the elevator!

In other situations without a natural closing, you may need to think more carefully about ending the conversation. In the United States, for example, people do not suddenly say good-bye and walk away. In fact, this way of ending a conversation may seem very rude. Politely ending a conversation actually involves three brief steps: signaling the end, ending, and taking leave.

CLOSING A CONVERSATION

Signaling the End

Well, [pronounced in a long, drawn-out way] . . . .

So, [also pronounced in a long, drawn-out way] . . . .

Well, okay, ...

Well, listen, ...

Look at the time!

Well, I know you're busy.

Ending

I should be going.
I'm afraid I have to leave now. It's getting late.

I have to {
get back to work.
meet someone.
get to class.
}

I'll let you get back to work now.

Taking Leave

Good-bye.

See you {
later.
in class.
tomorrow.
soon.
}

Activity 11:   Practicing a Conversation

1. Work in a small group of three people. Two of you will carry on a conversation, while the third person acts as observer. The observer should fill in the chart in Activity 12.
2. Imagine that you and your partner have come to class early. Develop a two- to three-minute conversation of small talk with suitable topics. You will need to greet each other, open the conversation, have a short discussion, and then close the conversation.
3. When everyone has finished, change partners. Work through the same situation.
4. Change partners one more time, so all three of you act as observers. When you finish, each observer can discuss the chart he or she completed.
5. Discuss the following:

   - Was it easier to keep the conversation going the second or third time? Why or why not?
   - Which strategies were used most often to keep the conversation going?
   - What topics seemed the best for small talk?

6. As a follow-up, pairs of students may carry out further conversations of small talk. Assigned observers or the teacher may use the Conversation Evaluation Form in Appendix A.

Activity 12:   Observing a Conversation

As you observe the conversation in Activity 11, fill in the following chart. Write the names of the two speakers in the appropriate columns.

OBSERVATIONS	SPEAKER A	SPEAKER B
What strategies does each speaker use to keep the conversation going? If possible, write the expressions and/or questions used. Also, note the use of nonverbal behavior such as nodding.		
What topics does each speaker discuss?		

Pronunciation Practice

The Past Tense -ed Sound

The past tense of all regular English verbs is formed by adding the *-ed* (or *-d*) ending to the verb. While the spelling of these past tense forms is regular, the pronunciation varies.

To understand the different ways that the final *-ed* is pronounced, it is important to be aware of the difference between voiced and unvoiced sounds. The easiest way to hear this difference is to put your hands against your ears and make these two sounds:

Voiced: zzzzzzzzzzzzzzzz

Unvoiced: *sssssssssssssssss*

You can also feel the difference by putting your hand on your throat. With the voiced sound (*zzzz*), you should feel a vibration. This vibration will not occur with the unvoiced sound (*ssss*).

Activity 13:   Practicing Final *-ed* Sounds

Listen to Activity 13 on the tape. A speaker will pronounce all of the words listed in this activity. Repeat each word that you hear.

The past tense forms of regular verbs are pronounced in three different ways.

1. If the verb ends in a $/t/$ or $/d/$ sound, the *-ed* ending is pronounced as an extra syllable — $/id/$ (pronounced as the vowel sound in *bud* or *bid*):

need—needed	want—wanted
attend—attended	wait—waited
decide—decided	end—ended
start—started	add—added
invite—invited	visit—visited

2. If the verb ends in an unvoiced consonant (except $/t/$), the *-ed* ending is pronounced as $/t/$. In this case, do *not* add an extra syllable to the pronunciation:

wash—washed	laugh—laughed
like—liked	help—helped
talk—talked	stop—stopped
watch—watched	work—worked
walk—walked	finish—finished

3. If the verb ends in a vowel sound or a voiced consonant (except $/d/$), the *-ed* ending is pronounced as $/d/$. In this case, do *not* add an extra syllable to the pronunciation:

live—lived	close—closed
rain—rained	call—called
play—played	enjoy—enjoyed
show—showed	rob—robbed
open—opened	use—used

Activity 14:   Identifying Final *-ed* Sounds

Listen to Activity 14 on the tape. The speaker will pronounce a verb, followed by its past tense. To help you hear the past tense ending, the speaker will use the past form of the verb in a sentence. Circle the ending you hear.

1. /id/ /t/ /d/		**7.** /id/ /t/ /d/
2. /id/ /t/ /d/		**8.** /id/ /t/ /d/
3. /id/ /t/ /d/		**9.** /id/ /t/ /d/
4. /id/ /t/ /d/		**10.** /id/ /t/ /d/
5. /id/ /t/ /d/		**11.** /id/ /t/ /d/
6. /id/ /t/ /d/		**12.** /id/ /t/ /d/

Activity 15:   Identifying Correct Pronunciation

Listen to Activity 15 on the tape. In each item the speaker will say a sentence and then repeat it. The pronunciation of the past tense verb in italics may be correct or it may be incorrect. If the past tense is pronounced correctly, put a check in the column labeled *Right*. If the past tense is pronounced incorrectly, put a check in the column labeled *Wrong*. Notice that in all of these sentences, the past tense requires an added /id/ sound.

SENTENCES	RIGHT	WRONG
1. Don *attended* class yesterday.		
2. Laura *needed* some help.		
3. The meeting *ended* at noon.		
4. Class *started* on time.		
5. Alice *wanted* to leave.		
6. Jeff *decided* to move.		
7. Louise *invited* me to the party.		
8. My boss *waited* for an hour.		
9. The teacher *handed* out the exams.		
10. Pat *completed* the form.		

Activity 16:   Practicing Correct Pronunciation

Listen to Activity 16 on the tape. The speaker will pronounce each of the sentences in Activity 15 *correctly*. Repeat each sentence after the speaker.

Activity 17:   Practicing Past Tense Verbs in a Story

1. Work individually. Think of a movie that you have enjoyed in English or your native language. Plan a brief summary of the story using the past tense: What was the name of the movie? Who were the main actors? Where did the story take place? When did it take place? Who were the main characters? What happened? What did you especially like or dislike about the film: the story, the actors, the photography, the music, etc.? You may write brief notes, but do not write out your report.
2. Work in a small group or as a class. Take turns giving your movie reports. Be sure to tell the story in the past tense. Pay careful attention to the correct pronunciation of the past tense endings of the regular verbs.

Learning Strategies

Expanding Vocabulary

Many students of English are concerned about their lack of vocabulary. After considering the strategies for vocabulary building that are listed in Activity 18, make a plan for organizing your vocabulary learning.

Activity 18:   Building Vocabulary

1. Work individually. Think about the strategies used for learning or studying vocabulary words. In the column labeled *You*, use the following key to indicate how often you use these strategies:

   + = frequently   √ = sometimes   − = never

METHODS	YOU				
A. Write the word several times					
B. Use the word as much as possible					
C. Say the word aloud several times					
D. Repeat the word silently					
E. Write the word and its translation in a list					
F. Write the word with its meaning or a synonym in English					
G. Connect the word with a picture or a drawing					
H. Write and memorize a sentence that includes the word					
I. Work in a group to practice and test meanings of words studied in class					

METHODS	YOU				
J. Test yourself from a list of words by covering up the meanings					
K. Make flash cards with the word on one side and its meaning on the other					
L. Make an audio recording of words with their meanings or synonyms, and then listen to the tape					
M. Make an audio recording of sentences or stories that contain new words, and then listen to the tape					
N. Underline new words in readings, and, using a dictionary, write their meanings in the margin					
O. Try to figure out the meaning of new words in readings from the context					
P. Other:					

2. Work in a small group of three or four people. Write each person's name at the top of a column in the chart. Exchange information so you can fill in the chart.

3. Work together to prepare a short report of your group's results to the class. Discuss the following:

   • What are the most common methods that members of your group use to learn new words?
   • Which methods seem the most successful? Which seem the most interesting?
   • Which new methods do members want to try?
   • Are there some methods that no one in your group uses or wants to try? If so, why not?

4. When all the groups have finished, present your reports to the class.

Cross-Cultural Communication

Considering Nonverbal Communication

People often communicate without words by using their hands, arms, face, or other nonverbal methods of communication. This nonverbal communication, however, is not the same in all countries. If students in your class come from different countries or cultures, you may want to compare ways that you communicate certain messages nonverbally.

Activity 19:   Discussing Nonverbal Communication

1. Work in a small group. Each person should choose several of the following messages. Take turns sending these messages nonverbally, while the other group members guess what you mean.

   A. Hello. (to someone across the room)
   B. Good-bye.
   C. Come here.
   D. Yes./I agree.
   E. No./I disagree.
   F. I don't know. I have no idea.
   G. Wait a second. I'm trying to think.
   H. Good luck.
   I. It's okay.
   J. That's very expensive.
   K. I can't hear you.
   L. Shhhh. Be quiet.
   M. It's time to leave.
   N. Stop! Don't come closer.
   O. You did a great job! It was a success.
   P. Calm down! Don't be upset.
   Q. What do you think?

2. As a group, discuss the following:

   • Within your group, how many different ways can you find to communicate each message? Does everyone understand each way?
   • If group members come from different countries, which messages might cause confusion?

3. When all the groups have finished, share your ideas as a class.

Unit 3
Speaking to a Group

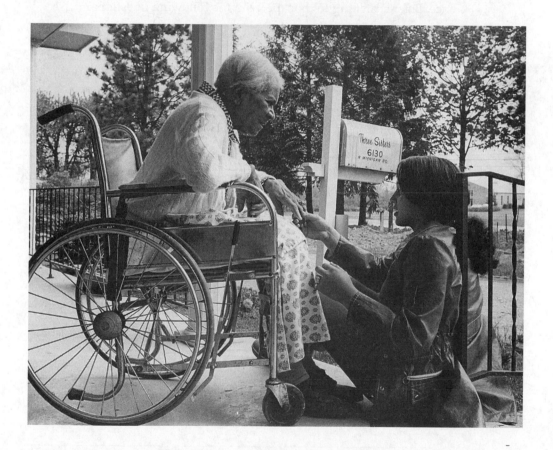

- Describe the scene in the photograph.
- Have you ever done any kind of volunteer work?
- Can you think of other kinds of volunteer work?
- Why do you think people volunteer to help others?
- What reasons do people have for *not* doing volunteer work?
- What are ways to encourage people to do volunteer activities?

Listening Practice

Activity 1: Listening to a Story

1. In this activity you will hear a speaker talking about a personal experience. Before listening to the tape, read the following questions:

    A. Where did the story take place?

    _____

    B. Why was the road so dangerous?

    _____

    C. What could the passengers see below?

    _____

    D. Why did the bus driver have to drive the bus so close to the edge of the road?

    _____

    E. What happened to the back left wheel of the bus near the top of the mountain?

    _____

    F. What did the passengers on the bus do to make the situation even worse?

    _____

    G. What did the passengers on the bus do that saved the situation?

    _____

    H. What did the passengers on the other bus do to help?

    _____

    I. What happened to the road two days after the speaker's trip?

    _____

    J. How did this experience make the speaker feel?

    _____

2. Now listen to Activity 1 on the tape. Answer the questions according to the information you hear.

3. Work in a small group or as a class to compare your answers.
4. Work with a partner. Take turns retelling this story to each other.

Activity 2:   Identifying Expressions Showing Time Order

1. Before doing this activity, review the expressions that show time order in the box "Telling a Story" in this unit.
2. Listen to Activity 2 on the tape. You will hear sentences from the story in Activity 1. Write the time expression the speaker uses in each one.

A. _____

B. _____

C. _____

D. _____

E. _____

F. _____

G. _____

H. _____

I. _____

J. _____

3. Work in a small group or as a class to compare your answers.

Activity 3:   Listening to a Talk

1. Work in a small group. Think about the advantages of working in a small group to improve your speaking and listening skills in English. List several of the most important advantages:

A. _____

B. _____

C. _____

D. _____

2. Now listen to Activity 3 on the tape. As you listen, put a check next to the advantages you listed that are the same as those you hear.
3. Listen to Activity 3 again. As you listen, fill in the blanks with the words you hear.

During this course, you will be participating in many small group activities. Today, I'd like to explain four main advantages of working in a small group to improve your speaking and listening skills in English.

The _____ main advantage of group work is that it gives students more language practice. In other words, students working in a group have more opportunities to practice speaking than in a class led by a _____. Group work gives students a chance to use the skills, structures, and vocabulary that they are learning in class. This is _____ because people can't learn a language simply by studying rules or memorizing vocabulary lists. If students get more practice, then they can _____ faster progress in learning the language.

Another important advantage of group work is that many students feel more comfortable speaking in a group rather than in front of the entire class. For _____ , many students feel nervous when the teacher calls on them to speak in class. They worry about making a _____ in front of so many people. In a small group, however, students don't worry as much about making mistakes, so they participate more actively and more comfortably. If students _____ more comfortable, then they participate more. As a result, they can _____ more.

The third main advantage of group work is that it encourages students to share their _____ and knowledge. Group members learn to cooperate and to help each other. For example, if a student has _____ expressing an idea, that student can ask another group member for help instead of asking the teacher. This

_____ that group members can take more responsibility for their own learning because they do not have to depend on the teacher for all their information. This is _____ because experts say that students learn more when they are actively involved in the learning process.

_____, the fourth main advantage of group work is that it helps students develop important _____ skills. For instance, in a group discussion, students practice taking turns, asking questions, agreeing, disagreeing, and so forth. This type of practice is important _____ it prepares students for using English in real-life situations.

In conclusion, then, I believe that group work has _____ important advantages. These are: one, more language practice; two, a more comfortable class atmosphere; three, more learner involvement; and finally, _____ for the real world.

4. Work in a small group or as a class to compare your answers.

Activity 4:   Putting a Presentation Together

1. Work with a partner. Review the expressions listed in the boxes "Including Specific Information" and "Putting Your Ideas Together" in this unit. Now review the text of the presentation in Activity 3.

   A. Draw a line under the expressions that connect the main ideas and that conclude the presentation.
   B. Circle the expressions that introduce an example.
   C. Draw a double line under the expressions that introduce an explanation.
   D. Put a box around the expressions that introduce a reason.
   E. Draw a wavy line under the expressions that express a consequence.

2. Work in a small group or as a class to compare your answers.

Communication Skills

In this unit, you will start building the skills you need to feel comfortable speaking to a group. You will deal with more formal presentations in Unit 5.

Building Confidence

Do you get a terrible feeling of fear or nervousness when you have to speak in front of a group of people? If you do, you are not alone. In fact, you belong to the majority of people who suffer from *stage fright*. Although stage fright can cause great anxiety, it can also give you a certain energy that you can put to positive use. You might try the following ways to reduce your stage fright when speaking before a group:

- Choose a topic that you know and that interests you.
- Give yourself enough time to prepare and organize the presentation.
- Practice in advance.
  —Make and analyze an audio or video recording of your presentation.
  —Rehearse your presentation in front of friends, family, or a mirror.

- Take some time to relax immediately before you begin to speak.
  —Pause a few seconds.
  —Establish eye contact with your listeners.
  —Take one or two deep breaths before speaking.

In general, the best way to build your confidence is to practice. In fact, the more time you spend rehearsing, the better your presentation will be. You can practice in front of your family, your friends, or even a mirror. Another excellent way of practicing is to make a recording of your presentation. You can listen for problems and then work on improving them before you speak to the group. In any case, practicing gives you a chance to gain confidence and to make sure that your presentation meets the time requirements.

TELLING A STORY

When you tell a story, you need to help the listeners follow your progress as you move from one event to another.

Introducing Your Story

Provide a brief introduction to explain why you want to tell this story.

I'd like to tell you about a very strange experience I had last summer while I was traveling in Canada.

Showing Time Order

First, . . .
Second, . . .
Third, . . .
Next, . . .
Then . . .
Later, . . .
After that, . . .
Finally, . . .

A few days ⎱
Several hours ⎰ later, . . .

During the ⎰ trip . . . .
          ⎱ party . . . .

The following ⎰ day . . . .
            ⎱ month . . . .

Concluding

Signal the end. Then repeat or review the significance of the event.

So, to end my story, it was a very difficult trip, but I think I learned how to take care of myself in an emergency.

Do not end by saying suddenly, "That's all," or "I'm finished."

Activity 5:   Choosing a Topic for a Talk

1. Work individually. Choose one of the following topics for a three- to four-minute talk:

   - An interesting, exciting, funny, frightening, or dangerous experience
   - A favorite family story, perhaps about an event that happened to a family member
   - An important or special event from your childhood
   - A story you have read, seen on television, or heard from a friend

2. Examine your topic more carefully:

   - Do you know or remember enough details to make your story interesting?
   - Can you tell the story in three to four minutes?

3. As you answer these questions, you may discover that you need to choose a different topic. You may have to work through several possibilities before you make a final decision.

Activity 6:   Planning a Talk

1. After you have chosen a topic, review the details that you want to include:

   - What exactly happened? Where? When?
   - Who was involved in the story? How did they feel? What did they think?
   - What made this event significant or memorable?

2. Consider how you will start and end your talk.

3. Practice telling this story to see how long it lasts. You may need to add or delete information to make it fit the time limit of three to four minutes.

Activity 7:   Practicing with a Partner

1. Work with a partner. Present your talk from Activity 6 to your partner, without stopping for questions or comments. Do not try to memorize or write out your story in advance. Your partner or the teacher should keep track of the time.
2. When you finish telling the story, your partner should retell it to you, as he or she has understood it. This retelling can help you see whether you have to change your story to make it clearer or easier to understand.
3. Switch roles so that your partner presents his or her story and you retell it. Again, be sure to note how long it lasts.
4. If necessary, add or delete information so your presentation meets the time limit. Also, make any other changes you feel are necessary.
5. When all the pairs have finished, change partners to tell your stories to a new person. Be sure that your talks meet the time limit.
6. Think about telling this story to a group or to the class as you work through the next section on delivering a presentation.

Improving Your Delivery

Delivery refers to the way you use your eyes, voice, and body to communicate your message. Of course, what you say is important, but the way you say it also has a strong effect on your listeners. Speakers in different cultures follow different customs when speaking to groups; however, you may find the following guidelines useful in this course:

1. *Eye contact* plays an essential role in keeping your listeners' interest. By moving your eyes from person to person, you can give listeners the feeling that you are talking to them as individuals. You can also see whether or not people are following your message by watching their faces. With a large group, you should move your eyes slowly from one section of the room to another as you are speaking. Be careful not to focus all your attention on only one person—such as the teacher—or on only a few people. You need to involve all the people in your audience by looking at them directly.

2. *Volume*—the loudness or softness of your voice—is important when speaking to a group. Your voice should be loud and strong enough to keep the interest of your listeners. Also, by raising or lowering your voice, you can emphasize certain points of your talk.

3. *A natural manner* of speaking will help to maintain your listeners' attention. You may feel nervous, but do not try to memorize or read your presentation. It is much more effective to use notes and to speak to people in a conversational manner.

4. *Posture*—the way you hold your body—conveys a message to your listeners. In general, you can express confidence by standing up reasonably straight with a relaxed posture.

5. *Movement* also has an effect on your listeners. For example, when standing in front of a group, you may want to take a few steps one way or another. However, do not pace back and forth or sway from side to side while you are talking. These kinds of unnecessary movements can distract listeners from your message.

6. *Hand or arm gestures* can be effective if you feel natural and comfortable using them. You may use gestures to emphasize a point or to describe something. In general, though, do not distract your listeners from your

message by playing with a pencil, pushing your hair off your face, folding and unfolding your arms, or doing anything else to draw attention to yourself.

Listeners can play an important role in making a speaker feel comfortable. When someone is speaking to a group, listeners should show their interest by:

- Looking directly at the speaker
- Nodding or smiling occasionally

Generally, you will be asked to stand in front of the class when giving a talk. However, in the next activity, you can sit in your seat as you become used to speaking to the class.

Activity 8:   Telling a Story to a Group

1. Work in a small group or as a class. Move your seats into a circle. Take turns telling the stories that you practiced in Activity 7. Try to meet the time limit of three to four minutes. Be sure not to memorize or write out your story in advance.
2. After everyone has finished, discuss the following as a class:

   - How did you feel speaking to the group or class?
   - Was it difficult looking directly at people as you were speaking?
   - Did the listeners try to make the speakers feel more comfortable?

Including Specific Information

People in academic and professional settings are often asked to give talks that provide information on a variety of subjects. In these situations, you can add interest to your topic by considering the following questions:

- What do you mean?
- For example?
- How?
- Why?
- So?
- So what?

Let's take a simple example to show how you can use these questions to develop an idea for a talk. Imagine that you are speaking on the important qualities that a teacher should have. One quality you might mention is patience. Let's see what you might say about patience.

Explanations

Explanations answer the question, "What do you mean?" In this case, what exactly do you mean by *patience*? You might explain that patience means the ability to accept pain or trouble without complaining or losing control. You could also say that patience means being able to deal with problems calmly, without being in a hurry.

Examples

Specific examples help answer the question, "For example?" To develop the idea of patience further, you need to think of specific situations in which teachers need patience. For example, teachers need patience to deal with slow learners. In such cases, teachers may take extra time in or out of class to help these students learn the material. In another example, teachers may need patience to deal with students who are not interested in the subject.

Anecdotes

Anecdotes are brief stories about you, your friends, your family, or other people you know. Anecdotes address the question, "For example?" In fact, listeners often remember something longer when it is explained with a personal story. You could easily develop the idea of patience by telling a story about a particular situation in which a teacher showed a lot of patience, how that made you (or another person) feel, and why that was important. This type of an anecdote illustrates your point and adds interest to your presentation.

Scenarios

Scenarios are another way to answer the question, "For example?" While an anecdote is a story about something that actually happened, a scenario is a story about something that *might* happen. In a scenario, you try to make a point by having your listeners imagine a particular situation. For example, in developing a scenario about patience, you could say, "Imagine that a teacher has several shy students. These students have a lot of useful ideas, but they feel too nervous to participate in class discussions. In this case, a patient teacher will be able to give them time to gain confidence in their speaking ability. Then, with enough time . . . ."

Concrete Details

Concrete details answer the question, "How?" You can make your examples, anecdotes, and scenarios more forceful by including concrete details. For instance, consider the example of a teacher trying to deal with students who are not interested in the subject. You can make this example stronger and more interesting by adding concrete details such as the following:

- *How* do these students act in class?
  —Talk to their friends
  —Don't do their homework
- *How* can the teacher deal with these students?
  —Show personal interest in each student
  —Help the students understand that the information in the course will be useful to them

These concrete details help your listeners really understand the quality of patience that is needed to deal with this type of problem.

Reasons

Reasons answer the question, "Why?" Why, for example, is it important for a teacher to be patient? You might say that it is important because students feel more comfortable with a patient teacher. Another reason might be that a patient teacher gives students time to think.

Consequences

You can consider consequences or effects in answer to the questions, "So?" or "So what?" One way to develop an idea is to keep asking yourself, "So what?" (Keep in mind that in normal conversation, the question "So what?" can sound very rude.)

A: If a teacher is patient, students feel more comfortable.
B: So what?
A: They participate more in class.
B: So what?
A: If students participate more in class, they become more involved in the lesson.
B: So what?
A: They learn more.

INCLUDING SPECIFIC INFORMATION

Giving an Explanation

Let me explain what I mean by . . . .
This means that . . . .
That is, ...
In other words, ...

Using an Example

Let me give you an example.
For example, ...
For instance, ...

Telling an Anecdote

Let me tell you a story to show what I mean.

Using a Scenario

Imagine that . . . .
Suppose that . . . .

Giving Reasons

The reason is that . . . .
This is important (necessary, a problem) because . . . .

Considering Consequences

If a teacher is patient, then students feel more comfortable.
As a result, ...
Therefore, ...
Consequently, ...

Activity 9:   Developing an Idea

1. Work in a small group. Think about another important quality that good teachers should have, such as a sense of humor, intelligence, kindness, or the ability to explain clearly.
2. Brainstorm ideas about this quality. Try answering the questions: *What do you mean? For example? How? Why? So? So what?* How can you use explanations, examples, anecdotes, scenarios, concrete details, reasons, and consequences to explain this quality? Each group member should write his or her ideas on a separate sheet of paper.
3. When all the groups have finished, share your ideas as a class.

Activity 10:   Developing Ideas with Specific Information

1. Work in a small group. Imagine that you are giving a talk on the following topic:

   The problems of traveling alone
   A. It can be lonely.
   B. It can be dangerous.
   C. It can be expensive.

2. Work together to find ways of developing each problem, using explanations, examples, anecdotes, scenarios, concrete details, reasons, and consequences.
3. Take notes on the ideas that you develop. Keep these notes because you will need them for Activity 19.
4. When all the groups have finished, share your ideas as a class. You may add ideas to your notes to use later.

PUTTING YOUR IDEAS TOGETHER

Here are some expressions that you might use in giving a talk on the problems people face when traveling alone. Of course, these are only some of the many possible expressions.

Introducing the Topic

Today I'd like to talk to you about several problems that people face when they travel alone.

Starting with the First Main Point

To start with, ...
The first problem is . . . .
First of all, ...

Adding Other Main Points

The second problem is . . . .
Another problem is . . . .
The final problem is . . . .

Concluding the Talk

In conclusion, because of these problems, I usually prefer to travel with at least one or two friends.

Speaking from Notes

Generally, the most effective way to speak to a group is in a conversational manner, using notes. The purpose of these notes is to help you remember your main points. You should not try to write out every word of a talk or to memorize it word for word. To help you remember the order of the main points you want to present, you can make brief notes on index or note cards. Consider the following guidelines when preparing such cards:

1. Buy a packet of index or note cards immediately. These cards are heavier and thus easier to use than cut-up pieces of regular paper. Do *not* write your notes on notebook paper.
2. Write only key words or short phrases to help you remember the order of your main points. You should be so familiar with the information that you need only to glance at these notes occasionally to refresh your memory.
3. Use one card for the introduction, one for each main point, and one for the conclusion. Be careful not to put too much information on each card.
4. Write your notes in dark pencil or ink. It is important for them to be neat and clear, so that you can easily read them.
5. Write on only one side of each card. This will make the cards easier for you to handle and refer to while you are speaking.
6. Number each card so that you do not lose your place.
7. If you want to emphasize something, underline it, write it in capital letters, or use a different color ink.
8. Use these cards when you practice, so you will be familiar with them.
9. When speaking, be sure not to distract your listeners by shuffling or playing with your cards.

Figures 1 and 2 are examples of the first two note cards you might use for an informal talk on problems that people face when traveling alone.

FIGURE 1

```
┌─────────────────────────────────────────────┐
│                                          ②   │
│   FEELING LONELY                              │
│                                               │
│   — In hotels                                 │
│                                               │
│   — In restaurants                            │
│                                               │
│   — Sightseeing                               │
│                                               │
│   — Can't share fun                           │
│                                               │
└─────────────────────────────────────────────┘
```

FIGURE 2

Activity 11:   Preparing Note Cards for a Talk

1. Work individually. Choose one of the following topics (or a similar one) for an informal talk of three to four minutes:

   • Advantages (or disadvantages) of being single, being married, having children, getting old, being a teenager, living alone, having a roommate, living in an extended family, living in a city, living in the country, doing volunteer work, exercising regularly, walking, owning a pet, reading a daily newspaper, subscribing to a particular magazine, traveling, etc.
   • Important qualities of a good friend, parent, boss, student, etc.

2. Plan a presentation on your topic, including specific information to support your ideas. Make note cards you can use in giving this talk.

3. When everyone has finished, exchange cards with another student. Discuss the following:

   • Do the notes include only key words or short phrases (not sentences)?
   • Do the notes seem easy to read? Is the writing dark enough?
   • Are the cards numbered?
   • Are the notes written on only one side of each card?

4. If necessary, make new note cards for your talk.

Activity 12:   Giving an Informal Talk

1. Work with a partner. Use the note cards you made in Activity 11 to practice giving your talk. Make sure that it meets the time limit of three to four minutes.
2. Work in a group or as a class. Take turns giving your talks.
3. Listeners may fill out an observation card for each speaker according to the instructions in Activity 13.
4. Assigned observers or the teacher may use the Presentation Evaluation I Form in Appendix A.

Activity 13:   Observing the Talk

1. As you listen to each speaker, consider the delivery style.
2. Use the following key to evaluate each speaker:

   + = very good   √ = satisfactory   – = needs more practice

   _____ **A.** Maintained eye contact with listeners in all parts of the room

_____ **B.** Spoke loudly and clearly

_____ **C.** Spoke in a natural, conversational manner

_____ **D.** Posture, movement, gestures showed confidence, and did not distract listeners

_____ **E.** Used notes effectively (if applicable)

2. For each speaker, use an index or note card to make an evaluation form as follows:

```
┌────────────────────────────────────────────────────┐
│                                                      │
│   Name of Speaker: _____      │
│                                                      │
│   A. _____       Comments:                           │
│                                                      │
│   B. _____                                           │
│                                                      │
│   C. _____                                           │
│                                                      │
│   D. _____                                           │
│                                                      │
│   E. _____                                           │
│                                                      │
└────────────────────────────────────────────────────┘
```

Write comments on this card that you think might help the speaker in planning future talks.

3. When all the speakers have finished, give each one your evaluation.

Pronunciation Practice

The Final -s Sound

In English, you need to be careful to pronounce the -s at the end of:

- Present tense verbs in the third-person singular
  Mary seldom watches television.
  The manager writes several reports each week.
- Plural nouns
  I attended several meetings.
  The teachers had a conference.

- Possessives
    I heard the student's presentation.
    What is the speaker's problem?

Activity 14:   Practicing Final -s Sounds

The final -s sound is pronounced in three different ways. Listen to Activity 14 on the tape. A speaker will pronounce all the words listed to demonstrate these three sounds. Repeat each word.

1. The final -s may be pronounced as a separate syllable that sounds like /iz/. This happens when the final sound of the word is /s/, /z/, /ch/, /sh/, /zh/, /ks/, or /j/.

watch—watches	speech—speeches
teach—teaches	course—courses
notice—notices	box—boxes
wash—washes	class—classes
pronounce—pronounces	language—languages
choose—chooses	size—sizes
judge—judges	bridge—bridges
miss—misses	quiz—quizzes

2. The final -s may be pronounced as an unvoiced /s/ sound when the word ends in an unvoiced consonant (except the /s/, /sh/, /ch/, or /ks/ sounds listed in item 1). In this case, do *not* add an extra syllable.

get—gets	book—books
speak—speaks	month—months
make—makes	sport—sports
want—wants	test—tests
cost—costs	desk—desks

3. The final -s may be pronounced as a voiced /z/ sound when the word ends in a vowel or a voiced sound (except the /z/, /zh/, or /j/ sounds listed in item 1). In this case, do *not* add an extra syllable.

wear—wears	law—laws
go—goes	day—days
feel—feels	problem—problems
answer—answers	hobby—hobbies
see—sees	expression—expressions

Activity 15: Identifying Final -s Sounds

Listen to Activity 15 on the tape. The speaker will pronounce a word, followed by the same word with an -s ending. Circle the ending you hear.

1. /iz/ /z/ /s/
2. /iz/ /z/ /s/
3. /iz/ /z/ /s/
4. /iz/ /z/ /s/
5. /iz/ /z/ /s/
6. /iz/ /z/ /s/
7. /iz/ /z/ /s/
8. /iz/ /z/ /s/
9. /iz/ /z/ /s/
10. /iz/ /z/ /s/
11. /iz/ /z/ /s/
12. /iz/ /z/ /s/

Activity 16: Identifying Correct Pronunciation

Listen to Activity 16 on the tape. In each item the speaker will say a sentence and then repeat it. The pronunciation of the final s sound of the word in italics may be pronounced correctly or it may be missing. If the final s sound is pronounced correctly, put a check in the column labeled *Right*. If the final s sound is missing, put a check in the column labeled *Wrong*.

SENTENCES	RIGHT	WRONG
1. The *buses* are late.		
2. Mike often *misses* the bus.		
3. The sun *rises* in the east.		
4. Rita often *watches* TV.		
5. Those new *dresses* are expensive.		
6. Two *classes* were canceled yesterday.		
7. Fran read ten *pages* last night.		
8. Water *freezes* at 32 degrees Fahrenheit.		
9. I speak several *languages*.		
10. Dr. Smith *teaches* class at 8:00.		

Activity 17:   Practicing Correct Pronunciation

Listen to Activity 17 on the tape. The speaker will pronounce each of the sentences in Activity 16 *correctly*. Repeat each sentence after the speaker.

Activity 18:   Practicing Final *-s* Sounds

1. Work with a partner. Take turns interviewing each other using the following questions. In both interviews, the person asking the questions should read from the book and take brief notes on the answers. The person answering the questions must close the book to *listen* to the questions.

Speaker A Asks Speaker B:

- What time do you get up? Do you have an alarm clock, or does someone wake you up? Do you have trouble waking up?
- What do you do first, second, next, then?
- Do you eat breakfast? If so, what do you eat and drink? Do you fix it, or does someone else prepare it?
- When do you leave the house?
- How do you get to school or work? How long does it take to get there?
- How do you feel when you get to school or work?

Speaker B Asks Speaker A:

- What do you usually do at school or work?
- What time do you usually leave school or work?
- How do you get home? How long does it take?
- What time do you get home?
- How do you feel when you get home? What do you do first?
- What time do you eat dinner? Who usually cooks?
- How do you usually spend your evenings?
- What time do you usually go to bed? How long do you sleep?

2. Work in a small group or as a class. Take turns telling about your partner's routine morning or evening. Pay careful attention to the correct pronunciation of the final *-s* sounds.

Learning Strategies

Focusing on Fluency

In speaking, your main goal should be to make your meaning clear. An important aspect of getting your message across is *fluency*. Fluency refers to speaking smoothly with as few hesitations and repetitions as possible. Of course, even native speakers do not always speak smoothly. They hesitate at times as they are speaking. They also use fillers such as "you know," "ummm," "er," and "okay" as they are trying to think of what to say next. To sound fluent, however, you need to avoid long or unexpected pauses that interrupt the flow of your ideas. Furthermore, you should try to limit your use of fillers, since they can be very distracting to your listeners.

Activity 19:   Making a Recording

1. Work individually or with a partner. If possible, do this activity at home or in the language laboratory outside of class. Since this activity involves making an audio recording, you will need a cassette tape recorder, a microphone (if necessary), and a blank audiotape.
2. Plan a three- to five-minute presentation on the topic discussed in Activity 10: several problems that people face when they travel alone. You may use the notes you made in Activity 10, but do not write out your talk.
3. When you feel prepared, make a recording of your presentation. You may refer to your notes, but do *not* read your talk. Do the best you can, but do not worry if you make mistakes.
4. Listen to your recording, and answer the following questions:

   - Did you speak loudly and clearly?
   - Did you speak in a natural, conversational way, not reading or reciting your presentation from memory?
   - Did you speak smoothly, without too much hesitation or repetition?

5. Save the first recording of your talk. Then, record yourself giving the same presentation a second time.
6. Listen to and compare both presentations. Is the second one better than the first? If so, in what ways? If you are not satisfied with your improvement, make a third recording.
7. Write your name and date on the tape, and give it to your teacher for comments.

Cross-Cultural Communication

Explaining Proverbs

Proverbs are short sayings that people have handed down by word-of-mouth from generation to generation. Generally, proverbs offer advice, give warnings, or present an observation about life. They often reveal important cultural values or principles.

Activity 20:   Explaining Proverbs

1. Work in a small group. Read the following proverbs. Next to each, write the letter of the best explanation from the list following the proverbs. Before you begin, review the vocabulary words.

Vocabulary

bush = a low plant (like a small tree)
curiosity = interest in learning about something new
fence = a structure that divides or encloses property
glitters = shines brightly
haste = hurry or speed
leap = jump
leopard = a large, catlike animal with a yellowish coat and round, dark
           spots
stones = small rocks
worm = a small, boneless creature that birds eat

Proverbs

_____   **1.** Don't put all your eggs in one basket.

_____   **2.** Blood is thicker than water.

_____   **3.** A leopard can't change its spots.

_____   **4.** There's no use in crying over spilled milk.

_____   **5.** While the cat's away, the mice will play.

_____   **6.** Haste makes waste.

_____ 7. The grass is always greener on the other side of the fence.

_____ 8. Look before you leap.

_____ 9. Rome wasn't built in a day.

_____ 10. People who live in glass houses shouldn't throw stones.

_____ 11. All that glitters is not gold.

_____ 12. A bird in the hand is worth two in the bush.

_____ 13. No pain, no gain.

_____ 14. Curiosity killed the cat.

_____ 15. The early bird catches the worm.

Explanations

A. People with faults should be careful about criticizing the faults of others.

B. You shouldn't judge the value of something by its appearance.

C. We often feel that something we don't have is better than what we have.

D. You can't expect to get what you want without hard work.

E. It's better to be satisfied with something small that you have than to risk losing it by trying to get something bigger or better.

F. Family relationships are more important than other relationships.

G. The best way to succeed is by starting before the usual or expected time.

H. You shouldn't continue worrying about something that happened in the past because it's impossible to change it.

I. You can get into trouble if you try too hard to get information about something.

J. Before you act, you should consider the possible consequences.

K. If you hurry too much, something will probably go wrong.

L. It's risky to put all your hopes, efforts, or money on a single person or thing. If you lose that person or thing, you will lose everything.

M. You need to be patient to see the results of your work.

N. When the person in authority is not present, others will take advantage of the situation by doing things they wouldn't do if he or she were there.

O. It's almost impossible for people to change.

2. When all the groups have finished, compare your answers as a class.

Activity 21:   Explaining a Proverb

1. Work individually. Choose one of the proverbs in Activity 20 that you believe is true. Plan a two- to three-minute story that illustrates its truth.
2. Work in a small group or as a class. Take turns presenting your stories. You may use notes, if necessary, but do not read your story.

Activity 22:   Discussing Proverbs from Your Country

1. Work individually. Think of a proverb from your country. Translate it into English. Your translation does not have to be word-for-word, but it should convey the idea of the proverb as clearly as possible.
2. Work as a class. Take turns writing these proverbs on the board. Other students or the teacher can try to figure out what each proverb means. Be prepared to explain the proverb to the class.

Unit 4

Making a Group Decision

- Describe the scene in the photograph.
- Do you believe that people have a right to sleep in a park?
- Do you believe that the government has an obligation to keep city parks open to the public? Does the "public" include homeless people?
- Would you agree or disagree with a law that forbids people from sleeping in public parks? Why?

Listening Practice

Activity 1:   Identifying Rights and Obligations

1. Work in a small group. Consider the following situation and answer the discussion questions:

   Situation. Last week animal rights activists threw red paint on several women who were wearing fur coats. The activists did this because they believe it is wrong to kill animals in order to use their furs for coats or other clothing.

   Discussion
   • Do you think that people have a right to kill animals for their fur?
   • Do you think that people have a right to destroy other people's property as a protest?

2. Now listen to Activity 1 on the tape. You will hear five dialogues related to this situation. (You will hear each one twice.) Complete the following sentences according to the information in the dialogues. Before you begin, review the vocabulary words.

   Vocabulary
   activists = people who take action to support a strong belief
   protestors = people who are strongly against something
   cruelty to animals = causing animals pain or suffering
   ruin = destroy

   A. *Man*: People have a right to _____

   _____

   Woman: Protestors don't have a right to _____

   _____

   B. *Woman*: People have a right to _____

   _____

   Man: People have an obligation to _____

   _____

   C. *Man*: People have an obligation to _____

   _____

Woman: People have a stronger obligation to _____

_____

D. *Woman*: People don't have a right to _____

_____

Man: Protestors have an obligation to _____

_____

E. *Man*: People don't have a right to _____

_____

Woman: People have an obligation not to _____

_____

3. Work in a small group or as a class to compare your answers.

Activity 2: Identifying Expressions

1. Before doing this activity, review the expressions for agreeing and disagreeing in the box "Exchanging Opinons".
2. Listen to Activity 1 on the tape again. This time, for each dialogue, decide whether the second speaker agrees or disagrees with the first. Put a check in the correct column in the following chart. Then write the expression that the speaker uses to agree or disagree.

DIALOGUE	AGREE	DISAGREE	EXPRESSIONS
A			
B			
C			
D			
E			

3. Work in a small group or as a class to compare your answers.

Activity 3:   Listening to a Discussion

1. Work in a small group. Consider the following situation and answer the discussion questions:

Vocabulary

> *invasion* = interfering with or violation
> *investigation* = a careful study
> *undercover* = secret

Situation. In the past few years, television reporters have started using tiny hidden video cameras to carry out undercover investigations. In many of these investigations, the reporter takes on a false identity. For example, for one story a reporter got a job in the meat department of a grocery store. This reporter then took secret videos of the manager telling employees to put barbecue sauce on old, rotting meat so they could put it on sale again. Another reporter pretended to be a high school student for several weeks to get secret videos of students buying and selling drugs at school.

Discussion
- What other types of undercover investigations have you heard of?
- Do you think these types of investigations are a good idea? Why or why not?
- Do you think that reporters have a right to take secret videos of people who are breaking the law?

2. Now listen to Activity 3 on the tape. You will hear three people discussing this situation. Answer the following questions based on their discussion.

   A. The man believes that undercover investigations are an invasion of

   _____.

   B. What two expressions do speakers use to interrupt?

   _____

   _____

   C. What does one speaker say to keep her turn when someone tries to interrupt her?

   _____

D. What does one speaker say to get into the discussion?

_____

E. What does the final speaker say to end the discussion?

_____

3. Work in a small group or as a class to compare your answers.

Communication Skills

You may find yourself discussing *controversial issues* in many academic, professional, and even social situations. Controversial issues are those that cause conflict or disagreement because there are strong reasons to support opposing points of view. Issues that are currently considered controversial in the United States, for example, are:

- Should the military allow women in combat?
- Should doctors help terminally ill people kill themselves?
- Should abortions be legal?

These issues are considered controversial because there are strong arguments both for and against. You might compare them to issues that are *not* controversial:

- Should people drive when they are drunk?
- Should teenagers take illegal drugs?
- Should companies make products that can harm people?

These questions are not controversial because they do not cause reasonable, informed people to disagree. Someone (somewhere) might try to argue "yes" in response to one of these questions, but that would not be a normal response.

In the United States, an important academic, professional, and social skill is the ability to look calmly and fairly at opposing sides of controversial issues. Of course, you should be able to stand up for your beliefs. At the same time, though, you need to keep an open mind and give fair consideration to different points of view. Many teachers believe that discussions of controversial issues encourage students to explore new ideas and to develop their thinking and reasoning skills.

In taking a position on controversial issues, people often focus on:

- People's rights and obligations
- Important values
- Possible consequences of an action

Each of these points will be considered in much more detail in this and following units.

Considering Rights and Obligations

Many controversial issues involve a conflict over the rights and obligations that people have in certain situations. Of course, people usually have certain political and legal rights based on their countries' systems of government and law. In the United States, for example, people's rights include freedom of speech, freedom of the press, and freedom of religion. The details of these rights, however, are much too complex to explore here.

In general, most people believe in certain fundamental human rights. Two of these rights are:

- The right of every person to be treated with respect
- The right to personal freedom, to the extent that this does not interfere with the rights of others

Many controversies involve rights related to these, such as:

- The right to privacy
- The right to life
- The right to die
- The right to equal treatment

Activity 4:   Identifying Rights

1. Work individually. Decide whether you agree or disagree with each of the following statements. Put a check in the appropriate column to indicate your personal opinion. Your answers will depend on your own beliefs or principles. (Do not consider legal rights.)

STATEMENTS	AGREE	DISAGREE
A. People have a right to smoke wherever they want.		
B. Employers have a right to forbid employees from drinking alcohol during working hours.		
C. Students have a right to disagree with their teachers' opinions.		
D. People have a right to burn their national flag.		
E. Parents have a right to spank their children.		
F. All students have a right to free university education.		
G. Patients have a right to know if their doctor has AIDS.		
H. People have a right to buy as many handguns as they want.		
I. Parents have a right to limit the amount of television that their children watch.		
J. Students have a right to sleep in class.		

2. When everyone has finished, compare your ideas as a class.

In addition to rights, people have certain obligations to others. For example, people have legal obligations to others based on the law, contracts, or other formal agreements. People also have obligations based on their relationships with others. Some of these obligations include professional obligations (such as teacher to student or doctor to patient), business obligations (such as employer to employee or company to the public), family obligations (such as husband to wife, wife to husband, or parent to child), and personal obligations (such as friend to friend).*

Activity 5:   Identifying Obligations

1. Work individually. Decide whether you agree or disagree with each of the following statements. Put a check in the appropriate column to indicate your personal opinion. Your answers will depend on your own beliefs or principles. (Do not consider legal obligations.)

* Vincent Ryan Ruggiero, *The Art of Thinking: A Guide to Critical and Creative Thought*, 3rd ed. (New York: HarperCollins Publishers, Inc., 1991), p. 31.

STATEMENTS	AGREE	DISAGREE
A. Parents have an obligation to protect their children.		
B. Teachers have an obligation to like their students.		
C. Friends have an obligation to keep each other's secrets.		
D. The captain of a ship has an obligation not to leave a sinking ship before the passengers.		
E. Employees have an obligation to follow the rules of their company.		
F. Lawyers have an obligation to keep all information from their clients confidential.		
G. Police officers have an obligation to shoot criminals.		
H. Students have an obligation not to be rude to their teachers.		
I. Doctors have an obligation to tell their patients the truth.		
J. People have an obligation to keep their promises.		

2. When everyone has finished, compare your ideas as a class.

Exchanging Opinions

One of the most important principles of group discussion is equal participation. As a group member, you must take responsibility for successful group interaction by:

- Presenting your ideas
- Supporting your ideas with reasons, examples, and facts
- Asking others for their ideas
- Making sure that everyone participates

EXCHANGING OPINIONS

Asking for an Opinion

What do you think of . . . ?
How do you feel about . . . ?
What's your opinion of . . . ?

Giving an Opinion

In my opinion, ...
Personally, I think that . . . .
It seems to me . . . .
As far as I'm concerned, ...
As I see it, ...
I believe . . . .

Agreeing

That's right.
You're right.
I think so, too.
I agree with you.
I definitely agree.
I completely agree with you.

Expressing Reservations

Yes, but . . . .
Possibly, but . . . .
Yes, but the problem is . . . .

Disagreeing

I don't really agree with you.
I'm afraid I don't agree with you because . . . .
I'm not sure I agree with you. The reason is that . . . .
Yes, that may be true, but . . . .
Well, I can see your point, but . . . .
I see what you mean, but . . . .

Activity 6:   Discussing Rights and Obligations

1. Work in a small group. Discuss the following situations and reach agreement on a group answer to each question. Write one or two reasons to support your decision. During the discussion, be sure to practice different expressions for exchanging opinions.

    A. *Situation.* Elaine Franklin is shopping by herself in a large department store. She notices a woman shopping near her who seems to be very angry at her two-year-old child. Suddenly the mother starts slapping the child very hard in the face and shouting, "If you don't stop crying, I'll hit you even harder!" The young child screams, "Mama, stop!" and keeps crying. The woman starts to slap the child again. Ms. Franklin doesn't know the woman, but she is very worried about the child.

    Group Decision. Does Ms. Franklin have an obligation to try to stop the mother from hitting the child?

    _____ Yes   _____ No

    Reasons

    _____

    _____

    B. *Situation.* Many pedestrians have complained that beggars are becoming more aggressive and threatening as they demand money from passers-by. These beggars often stand at bus stops and block subway entrances, which makes it difficult for people to use public transportation. Store owners have also complained that beggars often stand on the sidewalk near their entrances. Shoppers don't want to pass beggars to enter these stores, so business owners are losing money. City officials have told police to begin arresting beggars.

    Group Decision. Do beggars have a right to beg in any public location?

    _____ Yes   _____ No

    Reasons

    _____

    _____

2. When all the groups have finished, compare your answers as a class.

3. Evaluate your participation by completing Activity 7.

Activity 7:   Evaluating Your Participation

1. Work individually. Consider your participation in Activity 6. Use the following key to answer the questions:

   + = frequently   √ = sometimes   − = almost never

   _____ **A.** Did you use different expressions for giving opinions, agreeing, and disagreeing?

   _____ **B.** Did you present and explain your ideas?

   _____ **C.** Did you ask others for their ideas?

2. How can you improve your participation in the next discussion?

   _____

   _____

Of course, many real-life situations involve a conflict between two or more rights and/or obligations. In such a controversial situation, you have to choose the right or obligation that is stronger or more important in this par-

ticular situation. If you feel that all the rights and/or obligations involved are equally important, then you should try to find a balance between them, if possible.

Activity 8:   Considering Conflicting Rights and/or Obligations

1. Work in a small group. Consider the following situations and reach agreement on a group decision. Half of the group members should take the position of one participant, while the other half should take the position of the other. Write one or two reasons to support your final decision. Be sure to consider the rights and/or obligations that are involved in the situation.

   A. *Situation*. A number of students in a public university have begun wearing T-shirts with disturbing messages. One message, for example, says, "Women Are Property." Other messages express hatred toward racial minorities. University officials are planning to ban these T-shirts. Some students have formed an organization, Students for Freedom, to protest this ban.

   Participants
   University officials
   Students for Freedom

   Group Decision. What action, if any, should university officials take?

   _____

   _____

   Reasons

   _____

   _____

   B. *Situation*. A five-year-old child has been in a terrible car accident. To give her a chance to live, the girl's physician must give her an immediate blood transfusion. However, both of the child's parents belong to a religion that forbids members from receiving blood transfusions, even in a life-or-death situation. With their strong religious beliefs, the parents refuse to give permission for a transfusion.

   Participants
   Representatives of the physician
   Representatives of the parents

Group Decision. What action, if any, should the child's physician take?

_____

_____

Reasons

_____

_____

2. When all the groups have finished, compare your final decisions as a class.

Considering Values

Controversial issues often force people to examine their *values.* Values are ideas or concepts that people consider to be important. Generally, people try to act according to certain positive values. That is, they try to be:

- *Fair,* by treating all people equally
- *Honest,* by telling the truth
- *Loyal,* by showing support and by being faithful to family, friends, employer and/or country.
- *Compassionate,* by trying to stop the suffering or pain of other people
- *Tolerant,* by recognizing and respecting opinions, practices, beliefs, or customs that are different from their own

In many situations, these values may conflict, and you will have to choose those that you consider to be the most important.

IMAGINING ANOTHER PERSON'S POSITION

In discussions, speakers often use a structure called the *unreal conditional* to consider what they would do in certain situations. Consider the following situation: During an exam, a teacher sees a student copying answers from the person next to him. The teacher immediately takes the test away from the student and gives him an *F* on the test. Some possible reactions to this situation, using the unreal conditional structure, are:

If I *were* the teacher,
- I *would do* the same thing.*
- I'd *warn* the student first.
- I *wouldn't give* the student an *F*.

If I *saw* a student cheating, I'd *give* him an *F* on the test.
If I *caught* someone cheating, I *would talk* to the student privately.

*In informal usage, some people say, "If I *was* the teacher, I'd . . . ."

Activity 9:   Identifying Values

1. Work individually. Imagine that the people in the following situations are acting according to certain values they feel are important. First, write the value that you feel the person in each situation is following. (More than one value might apply.) Then, write what *you* would do in the situation.

   A. *Situation.* A man finds a wallet with $100 and no identification in an empty elevator in the library. He turns in the wallet to the library's lost-and-found office.

   Reactions
   - From the man's point of view, this action is _____.
   - What would you do if you were the man?

   _____

   B. *Situation.* Although a father is shocked to discover that his son has robbed a bank, he stands by him, pays for his lawyer, and gives him emotional support.

   Reactions
   - From the father's point of view, this action is _____.
   - What would you do if you were the father?

   _____

C. *Situation.* A young man's parents believe strongly that he should marry someone of his own religion. However, when he marries a young woman of a different religion, his parents welcome her warmly into the family.

Reactions
- From the parents' point of view, this action is _____.
- What would you do if you were one of the parents?

_____

D. *Situation.* A man borrows $100 from his father and another $100 from a close friend on the same day. After he receives his salary, he can only pay back a total of $100. Therefore, he pays each person $50.

Reactions
- From the man's point of view, this action is _____.
- What would you do if you were the man?

_____

E. *Situation.* When a five-year-old boy dies in a car accident, his parents donate his organs (heart, liver, and kidneys) to be used in transplants.

Reactions
- From the family's point of view, this action is _____.
- What would you do if you were one of the parents?

_____

F. *Situation.* A nineteen-year-old college student, still living at home, tells his parents that he is gay. At first, the parents are very upset by this news. However, they say that this has no effect on their love for their son. The son continues to live at home while he is attending college.

Reactions
- From the parents' point of view, this action is _____.
- What would you do if you were one of the parents?

_____

G. *Situation.* A manager is responsible for selecting an employee for promotion. One of the employees is a very close friend of the manager. However, she decides to promote another employee who is better qualified.

Reactions
- From the manager's point of view, this action is _____.
- What would you do if you were the manager?

_____

2. When everyone has finished, work in a small group or as a class to compare your answers.

Activity 10: Considering Different Views of Fairness

1. Work in a small group. Discuss the following situations and reach agreement on a group answer to each question.

A. *Situation.* Laura Rogers, a professor at a Canadian university, has a policy of giving students a grade of zero on any in-class quizzes or exams that a student misses because of an unexcused absence. According to her policy, the only excused absences are illness, religious holidays, or "emergencies." One of the students, Ahmed, has asked for an excused absence for tomorrow, when a quiz is scheduled. He says that he must go to the airport with his family to say good-bye to his brother who will be leaving for a year. Professor Rogers says that she cannot give Ahmed an excused absence for such a reason. Ahmed is very upset because he does not want a grade of zero on the quiz.

Discussion
- From Ahmed's point of view, is this a fair decision? Why or why not?

_____

_____

- From the professor's point of view, is this a fair decision? Why or why not?

_____

_____

Group Decision. What is the best way to deal with this problem?

_____

_____

Reasons

_____

_____

B. *Situation.* A country spends several million dollars each year supporting a public military college that is open only to males. College officials say that a males-only policy is important to develop strong lead-
ership skills. Recently, however, several highly qualified young
women have applied to the college, but were rejected. The country
does not support any females-only colleges.

Discussion
- From the women applicants' point of view, is the country's support
  of the college fair? Why or why not?

  _____

  _____

- From the college officials' point of view, is the policy fair? Why or
  why not?

  _____

  _____

Group Decision. What action, if any, should the government take?

_____

_____

Reasons

_____

_____

C. *Situation.* A small, private university in the United States forbids dating or romantic relationships between students and faculty members,
with no exceptions to this rule. A faculty member has fallen in love
with one of his former students. The young woman is still a student
at the university, but she is not taking any classes from this professor.
A top administrator has learned of this relationship, and has told the
professor that he must stop dating this student immediately or lose
his job.

Discussion

- From the professor's point of view, is this a fair policy? Why or why not?

  _____

  _____

- From the administrator's point of view, is this a fair policy? Why or why not?

  _____

  _____

Group Decision. What policy, if any, should the university have regarding romantic relationships between faculty members and students?

_____

_____

Reasons

_____

_____

2. When all the groups have finished, share your ideas as a class.

Activity 11:   Considering Conflicting Values

1. Work in a small group. Discuss the following situations and reach agreement on a group answer to each question.

   A. *Situation.* Patricia Adams has just found out that her husband, Dan Adams, has been stealing small amounts of money from his company for the past two years. Mrs. Adams has told her husband that he must stop immediately. Mr. Adams, however, says that the company will never catch him and that he can't stop right now.

   Discussion

   - What is the honest thing for Mrs. Adams to do?

     _____

   - What is the loyal thing for Mrs. Adams to do?

     _____

Group Decision. What should Mrs. Adams do?

_____

_____

Reasons

_____

_____

B. *Situation.* Sam Miller, a professor of education at a state university, has just finished calculating final grades. Dr. Miller gave an *F* to Miriam, one of his international students. As Dr. Miller announced in class, 60 percent is the passing grade, and Miriam had a 54 percent average. Unfortunately, she did poorly on several assignments, and failed a test and the final exam. She attended class regularly, but she had great difficulty understanding the material. Before Dr. Miller has to turn in grades, Miriam visits his office to ask him to give her a passing grade of *D*. She explains that she will lose her scholarship if she receives an *F*. She will then have to return to her country without her degree.

Discussion
- What is the honest thing for Dr. Miller to do?

  _____

- What is the compassionate thing for Dr. Miller to do?

  _____

Group Decision. What should Dr. Miller do?

  _____

  _____

Reasons

  _____

  _____

2. When all the groups have finished, share your ideas as a class.

Taking Turns

A very important skill in a discussion is efficient turn taking. This means that you need to know how to get your turn at speaking and also give others a chance to speak. One difficulty in taking turns is knowing when it is appropriate to interrupt. In general, once a person is speaking, that person is allowed to finish his or her turn. An interruption at the wrong moment can sound very rude. However, there are times in a discussion when interrupting may be acceptable. For example, you may not hear or understand something the speaker has said, or you may want to add a quick comment. Generally, it is not considered polite for two people to talk at the same time during a discussion in English. For that reason, you should stop talking almost immediately when someone interrupts you. However, if someone tries to interrupt you inappropriately, you also have a right to finish what you are saying.

TAKING TURNS

Getting Attention

To indicate that you want to speak, you can use nonverbal signals such as leaning forward or raising your hand. You can also gain the attention of the group members during a pause by saying:

May I Could I	ask a question? say something here? make a suggestion?
I have	a question I'd like to ask. a point I'd like to make.

Interrupting

If you feel that an interruption would be appropriate, you can wait for a pause in the conversation and then say:

Excuse me, but . . . .
Pardon me, but . . . .
Excuse me for interrupting, but . . . .
Sorry to interrupt, but . . . .

Keeping Your Turn

Excuse me, I'd just like to finish this point.
If you could wait for a second, I'm just about to finish my point.
Could I please just finish my point?

Continuing after an Interruption

Anyway, ...
As I was saying, ...
In any case, ...
So-o-o, ...
Going back to what I was saying, ...

Activity 12: Exchanging Ideas in a Group

1. Work in a small group with an observer. The observer should read Activity 13 and complete the form during the discussion.
2. As a group, consider the following situation. Half of the group members should take the position of one participant, while the other half should take the position of the other. Reach agreement on a group answer to the question. Be sure to state reasons to support your decision.

Situation. Two weeks ago, Tom Martin, five years old, accidentally shot and killed his ten-year-old brother. This happened while the boys were playing with a gun they had found in a bedside table in their parents' bedroom. The boys' father, Mr. Martin, told police he needed the gun for protection in his dangerous neighborhood. A week later, police arrested Mr. Martin because a new state law holds parents responsible for violent acts committed by their children. Under this law, Mr. Martin is responsible for his son's actions because he left the loaded gun within easy reach of his children. In fact, eight children under the age of twelve have died in this city in the past six months in similar accidents. Mr. Martin now faces the possibility of spending two to four years in prison for this crime.

Participants
Representatives of Mr. Martin
Lawyers for the state

Group Discussion. What punishment, if any, should Mr. Martin receive?

_____

_____

_____

Reasons

_____

_____

3. When all the groups have finished, discuss your ideas as a class.

Activity 13:   Observing the Discussion

1. As the observer, fill in the following chart as the group members discuss the situation presented in Activity 12. Put a check in the column labeled *Contributions* each time a member makes a contribution. When the group finishes the discussion, add the number of contributions each member has made.

GROUP MEMBERS	CONTRIBUTIONS	TOTAL NUMBER OF CONTRIBUTIONS

2. Consider the group discussion. Use the following key to answer the questions:

   + = yes, most of the time   √ = sometimes   − = no, almost never

   _____ **A.** *Participation.* Did all group members take an equal part in the discussion?

   _____ **B.** *Pace.* Did the discussion move along at the right speed, without long pauses between speakers?

3. When you have finished your observation, discuss your findings with your group.
4. Your teacher or other observers may use the Group Discussion Evaluation I Form in Appendix A.

Pronunciation Practice

Sentence Stress

Unit 1 dealt with the importance of stressing the right syllable in pronouncing a word. This is called *word stress*, or *syllable stress*. In learning to pronounce English, it is also necessary to consider *sentence stress*. English speakers tend to stress the important words in a sentence by:

- Saying them with more force
- Holding them longer
- Saying them at a higher pitch

Of course, in stressing words of more than one syllable, speakers stress the syllable that normally receives word stress. In general, there is a greater difference between stressed and unstressed words in English than in other languages. This alternation of stressed and unstressed sounds produces the rhythm of the English language. As a rule, speakers of English tend to stress content words and to unstress function words. Content words express meaning, while function words show grammatical relationships with other words in the sentence. Consider the following examples:

Content Words

- Nouns: *people, offices, John, Ms. Smith*
- Main verbs: *write, talking, went, told*

- Adjectives: *good, tired, angry*
- Adverbs: *slowly, carefully, very*
- Question words: *who, what, when, where, how*
- Negatives: *no, not*
- Reflexive pronouns: the *self* in *himself, herself*
- Numbers and other expressions of quantity: *ten, hundreds, many*

Function Words

- Personal pronouns: *it, he, she, us*
- Articles: *a, an, the*
- Prepositions: *on, in, at, of*
- Common conjunctions: *and, but, or*
- Relative pronouns: *that, which, who, whom, whose*
- Possessive adjectives: *my, your, our*
- Auxiliary verbs: *has, have, must, may, can*
- Forms of the verb *to be*: *am, is, was, were*

Activity 14:   Listening to Sentence Stress

Listen to Activity 14 on the tape. The sentences in each group have the same stress pattern, as diagramed. Listen carefully to the way the unstressed syllables and words are pronounced. Repeat each sentence after the speaker.

1.

I'm finished.
They're absent.
I'm sorry.
She's thinking.
You told me.

2. ● • ●

Please begin.
Take your time.
Go to class.
Joan was sick.
Where's your book?

3. • ● • ●

She sat at home.
We helped the boss.
They stopped to talk.
He lived in Spain.
They missed the bus.

4. • ● • ● •

You asked a question.
She watched the program.
He needs to practice.
She wrote a letter.
The train was early.

5. • ● • • ●

He started to leave.
We thought you were sick.
She asked me to stay.
I see what you mean.
He opened the door.

6. • • ● • • ●

We've decided to leave.
He explained it to Anne.
We agreed to the plan.
They discussed it with Frank.
You can talk to your boss.

Activity 15:   Identifying Sentence Stress

1. Work with a partner. Underline the content words in the following telephone conversations:

   A. *Woman:* Hello.
      Man: Hello. Is Bob there?
      Woman: No, I'm afraid he's not here at the moment. Would you like
                to leave a message?
      Man: Yes. Could you ask him to call Tom Pearson?
      Woman: Certainly. Does he have your number?

Man: Yes, he does.
Woman: Okay. I'll give him the message as soon as he gets home.
Man: Thank you very much. Good-bye.
Woman: Good-bye.

B. *Man:*   Hello.
Woman: Hello. May I speak to Susan?
Man: I'm afraid you have the wrong number.
Woman: Oh? Isn't this 555-2654?
Man: No, it isn't. It's 555-2653.
Woman: Oh, I'm sorry.
Man: That's okay. Good-bye.
Woman: Good-bye.

C. *Woman:* Hello.
Man 1:   Hello. May I speak to Daniel?
Woman: Yes, just a minute please.
Man 2:   Hello. This is Daniel.
Man 1:   Hi, Daniel. This is Ron.
Man 2:   Oh, hi, Ron. How are you?
Man 1:   Fine. Listen, am I catching you at a bad time?
Man 2:   Actually, we were just sitting down to dinner. Could I call you back when we've finished?
Man 1:   Of course. I'll talk to you later. Good-bye.
Man 2:   Good-bye.

D. *Woman:* [Recorded Message] Hello. I'm afraid I can't come to the phone right now. If you leave your name and phone number after the beep, I'll get back to you as soon as I can. [Beep]
Man: Hello. This is Jeff Walters calling. Kathleen, I need to ask you a question about work. Could you give me a call when you get home? Thanks.

2. Now listen to Activity 15 on the tape. Make sure that you have underlined the stressed words correctly.
3. Work with a partner. Practice reading these dialogues, making sure to stress the content words.

Activity 16:   Listening for Missing Content Words

1. Read the following passage, which has some content words missing. Listen to Activity 16 on the tape. You will hear a speaker reading this passage. As you listen, fill in the blanks with the content words you hear.

Government officials feel that it is _____ to start controlling population growth. The _____ for this is that the government simply cannot take care of the growing number of _____ in the country. Poverty, unemployment, and a lack of housing are just some of the serious _____ that people face. Therefore, officials feel that they must try to _____ the number of children that couples have. One action that the government has taken is to _____ laws that discourage families from having more than one child. For example, parents can send one child to school for _____, but then they must _____ very high fees for any other children in their family. These laws have caused a lot of _____ in the country. Many citizens believe that people have a _____ to have as many children as they want without government control. Government officials, on the other hand, believe that the government has an _____ to work for the greater good of society.

2. When everyone has finished, work in a small group or as a class to compare your answers.
3. Work with a partner. Take turns giving a summary of this passage in your own words, without looking at the book. As you are speaking, try to put the correct stress on the content words.

Learning Strategies

Assessing Your Progress

Take some time to consider how much progress you have made in your speaking and listening skills.

Activity 17:   Assessing Your Progress

1. How do you feel about your progress in speaking and listening to English so far in this course? Use the following key to complete the chart:

   + = satisfactory progress, but need a little more practice
   √ = some progress, but need much more practice
   − = little or no progress; need to pay special attention to improve this skill

SKILLS	PROGRESS
A. Participation in class	
B. Participation in conversations	
C. Participation in group discussions	
D. Giving oral presentations	
E. Pronunciation	
F. Fluency	
G. Listening comprehension	
H. Feeling confident about speaking	

2. Work in a small group. Discuss the following:

   • In which skills have members of your group made the most progress since the beginning of the term?
   • Which skills still seem to need the most work?

3. Spend a few minutes looking through your textbook. Think about the types of activities you have done in this course. In your group, discuss the following:

   • Which activities have you found the most useful?
   • Which activities have you enjoyed the most?

4. When all the groups have finished, share your ideas as a class.

| Activity 18: Planning Strategies for Improvement |

1. Work individually. What can you do inside and outside of class to improve your weakest speaking and listening skills?

   A. _____

   B. _____

   C. _____

   D. _____

   E. _____

2. Work in a small group to share your ideas.
3. When all the groups have finished, share your ideas as a class.

Cross-Cultural Communication

Considering Cultural Values

In this unit, you have discussed values such as honesty, fairness, and compassion. Of course, there are many other values that people believe to be important.

| Activity 19: Explaining Values |

1. Work individually. Which of the following values are important in your culture?

Respect for the old	Obedience to authority
Personal freedom	Time
Obedience to parents	Tradition
Hospitality	The group
Privacy	Generosity
Honor	Success
Cooperation	Competition

2. Be prepared to explain to a group or to the class two or three values that are important in your culture. Of course, you may choose other values not included in the list. Use examples and/or anecdotes to explain these values.
3. Are values changing in your country? That is, do teenagers and people in their early twenties have different values from people who are forty or older? If so, use examples and anecdotes to explain some of these differences.

Unit 5

Developing a Presentation

- Describe the scene in the photograph.
- Why do people choose to look like this?
- How do you feel about people like this?
- How would you feel if you were one of their parents?
- As a parent, how would you deal with a child like this?
- In what other ways do young people rebel against traditional society?
- In what ways is rebellion such as this bad? In what ways is it good?

Listening Practice

Activity 1:   Listening to a Presentation

1. Work in a small group. Consider the photograph and answer the following questions:

   - Have you seen panhandlers (beggars) on the street?
   - How do these people act?
   - Do you usually give them money? Why or why not?
   - In general, do you think people should give money to panhandlers? Why or why not?

2. Review the following outline of a presentation. The speaker is expressing a personal opinion on giving money to panhandlers.

Introduction

I. Panhandlers have taken control of the city.

   A. Panhandlers are everywhere.

   Examples: They're on sidewalks, in _____,
in public buildings, and in bus stations; they stand in front of
_____ and block entrances to the subway.

   B. They have become a serious social _____.

   C. Poor and homeless people need help.

   D. However, giving them money _____.

II. There are three reasons that people _____
to panhandlers.

Body

I. Giving money does not _____ panhandlers' real
problems.

   A. Many panhandlers suffer from mental illness,
_____ addiction, and alcoholism.

   B. They need to go to agencies that provide long-term
_____ for their problems.

   Examples: Job counseling, drug and alcohol rehabilitation

   C. Giving money discourages panhandlers from trying to get

   _____.

   D. You make their situation worse by giving money so they can buy
_____ or _____.

II. Giving money makes the streets more _____.

   A. Giving money encourages panhandlers to continue

   _____.

    B. Some panhandlers are quiet and polite, but others

       _____ money.

    C. Panhandlers scare people by shouting at them,

       _____ them, or blocking their way.

    D. Pedestrians are afraid to walk down the street.

    E. Some people believe panhandlers have a _____

       to stand in public places asking for money.

    F. However, city residents have a right to feel _____

       walking in the city.

III. Many panhandlers are able to work, but they are

    _____.

    A. They don't want to work hard for low pay, so begging is an easy

       way to get money without working.

    B. By giving money, you discourage panhandlers from

    _____.

    C. Some panhandlers have signs saying they are hungry, but

       when you give money, they buy cigarettes, alcohol, or

       _____ instead of food.

    D. You don't know which people put your money to good use.

Conclusion

    I. Panhandlers need help, but you shouldn't give money.

    II. Other ways to help them:

       A. Donate money to an organized charity.

       B. Donate your _____ by volunteering to work in

         a homeless shelter.

       C. Write to government officials to put pressure on them to

    _____.

3. Listen to Activity 1 on the tape. As you listen, complete the outline according to the information you hear.

Activity 2:   Focusing on Organization

1. Listen to Activity 1 on the tape again. As you listen, answer the following questions:

    A. How does the speaker try to get the listeners' attention in the introduction?

    _____

    _____

    B. What expressions does the speaker use to move from one main point to another? Write these expressions in the order that you hear them.

    _____

    _____

    C. What does the speaker say to show that the presentation is coming to an end?

    _____

    _____

2. When everyone has finished, work in a small group or as a class to compare your answers.

Communication Skills

This unit focuses on planning and organizing a presentation. As you work through the activities, start thinking about a topic you can use for a four- to five-minute presentation that will be assigned later in the unit.

Assessing the Speaking Situation

In starting to develop a presentation, you need to consider your speaking situation in terms of the following: selecting your subject, narrowing your subject to a topic, analyzing your audience, and meeting special guidelines.

Selecting Your Subject

At times, your teacher or boss may give you a subject or a choice of subjects for a presentation. In many cases, however, you will have some freedom of choice. When this occurs, you need to spend time thinking of a good subject. Be careful not to hurry through this step! At this stage, you must have an open mind and be willing to "play" with a number of subjects. When selecting a subject for a presentation, consider:

- Are you interested in the subject?
- Do you know enough about this subject?
- If you need additional information, do you have the ability, the time, and the resources to find this information?

Narrowing Your Subject to a Topic

In preparing a presentation, it is important to narrow your subject into a specific topic you can cover in the time available. For example, you might be asked to give a presentation on the subject of drug abuse. This, however, is a very broad area. You need to develop this subject into a specific topic, such as causes of teen drug abuse in the United States, consequences of drug abuse, ways to stop drug abuse, or types of drug abuse. In fact, one mistake that many inexperienced speakers make is to choose a topic that is much too broad. Here are three ways to begin limiting your subject to a specific topic with a clear, limited focus:

1. *Restricting your purpose:* In identifying a topic, ask yourself, "What exactly do I want to do in this presentation?" That is, what do you want your listeners to understand, to believe, to feel, or to do as a result of your presentation? In academic and professional situations, most speakers have one of two purposes: to inform or to persuade.

    If your purpose is to inform your listeners, you want them to understand and remember the information you present. In an informative presentation, your purpose may be to:

• Demonstrate	• Explain
• Inform	• Describe
• Summarize	• Give instructions
• Narrate	• Analyze
• Report	• Express feelings

    If your purpose is to persuade your listeners, you want them to agree with your point of view. In a persuasive presentation, your purpose may be to:

- Persuade
- Recommend
- Propose
- Change attitudes

- Evaluate
- Support
- Oppose
- Call to action

2. *Asking focus questions:* Focus questions can help you shape a broad subject into a specific topic. Consider the following list of questions, using your general subject in place of S. You should skip any questions that do not apply to your subject.

- What are the causes of S?
- What are the effects or consequences of S?
- What are the advantages or benefits of S?
- What are the disadvantages or drawbacks of S?
- What are the dangers of S?
- What are problems or difficulties associated with S?
- What are ways to prevent or reduce S?
- What are ways to encourage or increase S?
- What are the important qualities or characteristics of S?
- What are different types of S?
- What are reasons to support S?
- What are reasons to oppose S?

3. *Limiting the scope:* You can also narrow your subject by limiting the scope of your presentation. You can do this by including one or more of the following in your topic:

- A specific place: *in this city* or *at this school*
- A specific time: *recent advances* or *future developments*
- A specific number: *three main effects* or *four basic reasons*
- A specific type: *prescription drugs* (not *all drugs*)

Of course, it takes time to shape your ideas into the best possible topic. In planning your presentation, you may have to adjust your topic to suit your information, your time limits, and your listeners. As you develop your presentation further, you should feel free to rethink and change the focus of your topic.

Activity 3:   Identifying Topics with a Clear Focus

1. Work with a partner. Consider the following list of possible topics for a five- to ten-minute presentation. Put a check next to each topic that has a clear focus.

    _____ **A.** The high divorce rate in the United States

    _____ **B.** Several benefits of living together before marriage

    _____ **C.** World pollution

    _____ **D.** Consumer protection

    _____ **E.** The effects of noise pollution on people

    _____ **F.** The Amazon rain forest

    _____ **G.** Religion in the United States

    _____ **H.** Several ways that you personally can help the homeless

    _____ **I.** Free government medical treatment for all citizens

    _____ **J.** Several advantages of living in an extended family

    _____ **K.** Types of weekend activities that can be enjoyed for free

    _____ **L.** Three major benefits of a four-day work week

    _____ **M.** Four important qualities of good parents

    _____ **N.** Violence

2. When all the pairs have finished, work in a small group or as a class to compare your answers.

Activity 4:   Developing Topics with a Clear Focus

1. Work in a small group. Consider the following subjects. For each one, develop at least five possible topics with a clear, limited focus. Write your ideas on a separate sheet of paper.

   A. Television commercials
   B. Divorce
   C. Health care

2. When all the groups have finished, share your ideas as a class.

Analyzing Your Audience

In a speaking class, you may be unsure of your "real" audience—the teacher or the other students. Generally, you should speak to the other students since they form the majority of your audience. Before selecting a topic, try to find out what kind of information your listeners might find interesting, useful, or necessary. To analyze your audience, consider the following points:

1. *Background information:* What characteristics do your listeners share: nationality, field of study, occupation, age, sex, etc.? As much as possible, try to relate your message directly to their common characteristics.
2. *Current situation:* What goals, experiences, or problems do your listeners share? People are usually interested in topics that affect them directly: their work, school, hobbies, interests, health, family, friends, community, city, and so forth.
3. *Wants and needs:* What are your listeners' wants and needs? According to psychologists, many people want or need:

   - To have friends, family, romance, and companionship
   - To enjoy success—personally, professionally, emotionally
   - To be valued and appreciated by others
   - To have self-respect and self-confidence
   - To earn or save money
   - To be safe and secure
   - To save time and/or effort
   - To be happy

   Of course, these wants and needs vary from person to person, group to group, and culture to culture, so you should try to decide which of these apply to your listeners.

4. *Level of English:* If your listeners are mainly nonnative speakers of English, are they all at the same level of ability or of mixed abilities? To make your message clear, you need to use language that everyone can understand.

5. *Knowledge of the subject:* How much do your listeners already know about your proposed subject? What new information or insights can you provide? Clearly, you do not want to waste your listeners' time by repeating information they already know. Furthermore, you do not want to present a topic that is too technical or too specialized for them.

Meeting Special Guidelines

When planning a presentation, be sure to follow any guidelines you have been given, such as the following:

1. *Due date:* When exactly is the presentation due?

2. *Time limits:* What is the time limit? Can you speak longer than the maximum, or will you be cut off at the end of this time?

3. *Other guidelines:* Are there any other requirements that you should follow? For example, did your teacher assign a specific topic or purpose for your presentation (such as to explain a process), or ask you to hand in presentation notes?

Activity 5:   Analyzing Your Class as an Audience

1. Work in a small group. Use the following points to analyze your class as an audience:

   A. Background information

   _____

   _____

   B. Current situation

   _____

   _____

   C. Wants and needs

   _____

   _____

D. Level of English

_____

_____

2. When all the groups have finished, compare your results as a class.

Exploring Your Topic

To find out whether you have chosen a suitable topic, you need to spend some time exploring it further. Two strategies—listing and clustering—can help you remember or discover what you know about a topic. After using these strategies, you may discover that you want to use a different topic. That's great! You should always be searching for the best possible topic.

Listing

Listing is an individual brainstorming activity. The goal is to discover all the ideas you have on a particular topic. You can then select those ideas that you might use in your presentation. Here is how listing works:

- At the top of a sheet of paper, write the topic you want to explore.
- Set a time limit of five to ten minutes.
- Write every idea that comes to mind. Do not stop to consider whether each idea is good or bad, useful or not.
- Write quickly, using words or short phrases. Do not worry about grammar or spelling.
- Use your imagination, and let your ideas flow. List every idea that comes to mind!

At the end of the time period, stop to review the ideas you have listed. At this point you may want to:

- Cross out any ideas that do not seem to fit.
- Put a check next to the most useful or interesting ideas.
- Spend a few more minutes adding any new ideas that come to mind.

Imagine that you have decided to give a presentation on the disadvantages of living in a city. Here is a possible list of ideas that you might develop:

Disadvantages of Living in a City

Murders, robberies

Subway dangerous at night

Rents—very expensive

Can't afford to buy a place to live

No parking

Buses, streets are crowded

Rude, unfriendly people

Many accidents

Worry about being mugged

Dirty streets—litter

Too much noise

Not enough trees or flowers—concrete!

Crime

Traffic jams

Afraid to go out at night

Taxis are expensive

Homeless people on streets

Ugly buildings

Litter in street

Activity 6:   Practicing Listing

1. Work in a small group. Imagine that you are planning a presentation on the advantages of living in a city. Use a separate sheet of paper to list all the ideas on this topic that come to mind.
2. When all the groups have finished, share your ideas as a class.

Clustering

Clustering is a way of seeing possible relationships among your ideas. It is easier to use this strategy if you have some sense of the main points you want to present. Here is how clustering works:

- In a word or short phrase, write your topic in the middle of a sheet of paper. Circle this topic.

- Write the main points, each in a word or short phrase. Place these main points around the circled topic. Circle each main point and then use a line to connect each one to the topic in the center.
- Now think of supporting information (explanations, examples, details, etc.) that relates to each main point. Write these ideas around the related main point. Again, circle each idea and connect it to the related main point with a line.

Here is an example of clustering on the disadvantages of city living:

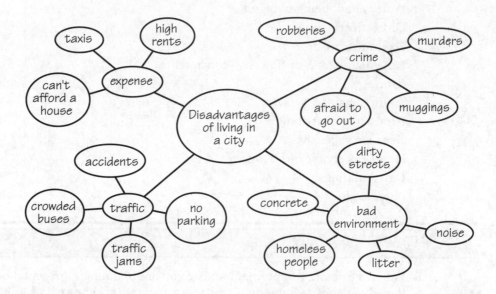

Activity 7:   Practicing Clustering

1. Work in a small group. Consider the topic that you worked on in Activity 6: the advantages of living in a city. Think of several main points that you might use to develop this idea, such as entertainment, cultural activities, educational facilities, and convenient transportation. Use a separate sheet of paper to try clustering your ideas.
2. When all the groups have finished, share your ideas as a class.

Organizing Your Ideas

After you have chosen a topic, you can begin developing the body, or main section, of your presentation. Basically, you develop the body by breaking down your topic into several main points. You then support each main point with specific information such as examples, explanations, facts, and details. In developing your topic, it is important to use from two to five main points. By limiting the number of main points, you will make it easier for listeners to understand and remember the information you present. If you use more than five main points, your listeners may have difficulty trying to follow your ideas. The following tree diagram shows an easy way to organize a presentation:

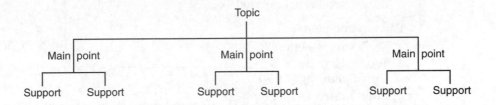

Many topics divide naturally into several main points: advantages, disadvantages, causes, effects, solutions, reasons, dangers, difficulties, ways, uses, qualities, types, stages, steps, categories, and so forth. In other cases, however, you may need to spend some time sorting through your ideas to organize them into two to five main points.

Grouping Ideas

If you used clustering as a strategy to produce ideas, then you have already started organizing. However, if you used listing, you first need to sort through all your ideas to identify the main points. Look back at the list of ideas on the disadvantages of living in a city. How can you organize all of these ideas into two to five main points? As you think about this, you should begin to see that some of the ideas are related. The way to start organizing is to put these related ideas into groups. For example, you might group the following—murders, robberies, worry about being mugged, crime, and afraid to go out at night—under crime, which could be one of your main points. You may need to cross out ideas that do not fit or that repeat other ideas.

As you begin to sort out your ideas, your notes might look like this:

Disadvantages of Living in a City

Crime
    Murders
    Worry about being mugged
    Subway dangerous at night
    Robberies
    Afraid to go out at night

Traffic
    No parking
    Traffic jams
    Many accidents
    Buses, streets are crowded

Bad environment
    Dirty streets—litter
    Too much noise
    Ugly buildings
    Litter in street
    Not enough trees or flowers—concrete!
    Homeless people on streets

Expense
    Rents—very expensive
    Can't afford to buy a place to live
    Taxis are expensive

By grouping ideas, then, you can identify a limited number of main points. In this example, the topic has been broken down into four main points: crime, traffic, bad environment, and expense.

At times, you may find it difficult to see ways of grouping your ideas. In these cases, it may help to consider certain broad categories that are often used as main points, such as the following:

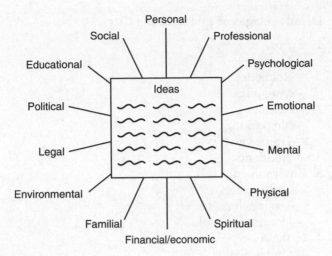

Outlining Your Ideas

It is much easier to make an outline after you have grouped your ideas. An outline helps you to get an overview of your presentation and to see whether you have enough information. As you are working on an outline, you can rearrange your ideas, include more information, or leave out some information. You may even decide to change your focus or your topic.

Two types of commonly used outlines are tree diagrams and informal outlines:

1. A *tree diagram* shows clearly how the topic is broken down into several main points. These points are then supported by more specific information.

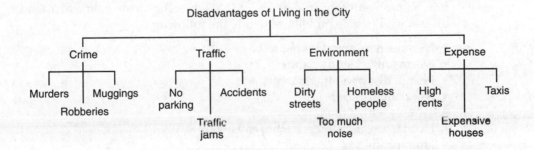

2. An *informal outline* shows the main points in a logical order, from most important to least important, or from least important to most important.

Disadvantages of Living in the City

1. Crime
   —Murders
   —Robberies
   —Muggings
2. Traffic
   —No parking
   —Traffic jams
   —Accidents
3. Environment
   —Dirty streets
   —Too much noise
   —Homeless people
4. Expense
   —High rents
   —Expensive houses
   —Taxis

Of course, in a presentation on the disadvantages of city living, you would use explanations, examples, anecdotes, consequences, and concrete details to explain each of the supporting points. Under homeless people, for example, you could give more details about the types of people you see, how you feel when you see them, and so forth. As you can see, it would be easy to transfer the information from this informal outline to note cards.

Activity 8: Organizing Ideas

1. Work with a partner. Imagine that you are planning to give a presentation on problems that students may face when they leave home to attend university. Possible problems include the following:

- Nervousness about taking tests
- Disorganized study habits
- Fear of disappointing parents
- Not enough sleep
- Trouble with a roommate
- Headaches and stomachaches caused by stress
- Homesickness
- Difficulty in taking class notes
- Not completing assignments on time
- Trouble with alcohol or drugs

- Waiting until the last minute to study for tests
- Difficulties in making friends
- Worries about girlfriends or boyfriends

2. One way to organize these ideas is to divide the topic into four types of problems: emotional, social, physical, and educational. Use a separate sheet of paper to make a tree diagram with these main ideas, listing the appropriate problems under each.

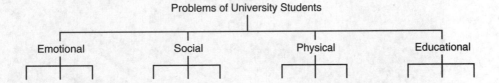

Problems of University Students

Emotional   Social   Physical   Educational

3. When all the pairs have finished, compare your tree diagrams as a class.
4. Use this information to make an informal outline.

Activity 9:   Outlining Ideas

1. Work with a partner. Imagine that you want to make a presentation on major causes of stress. Consider the following list of causes, in no particular order:

- Getting a divorce
- Having troubles with the boss
- Losing a lot of money in a bad investment
- Getting fired
- Getting married
- Retiring
- Receiving a promotion
- Purchasing a new home
- Having a son or daughter move away from home
- Buying a major item such as a car

2. What three or four main points could you use to organize these ideas in a presentation? You may find it helpful to refer to the diagram at the top of page 129.
3. Use a separate sheet of paper to make a tree diagram outlining these ideas.
4. When all the pairs have finished, compare your diagrams as a class.

When making a presentation, it is important to use transitions, or signals, to show how you have organized your ideas. Transitions are the words, phrases, or sentences that you use to connect your ideas in a clear and logical way. The use of transitions helps your listeners follow your progress as you move from one idea to another or from one part of your presentation to another.

USING TRANSITIONAL EXPRESSIONS

In presenting information, you need to be very clear in showing how your ideas logically fit together. Transitional expressions are like signs — they help the listeners to see where you are going in your presentation.

Starting with the First Main Point

To start with, ...
To begin, the first effect is . . . .
The first advantage is . . . .
Let's start with . . . .

Adding Other Main Points

The second main effect is . . . .
The next major cause is . . . .
Another serious problem is . . . .
In addition, ...
Furthermore, ...
The final way is . . . .

Providing Support

Let me give you an example.
An example of this is . . . .
For example, ...
For instance, ...
This is important because . . . .
As a result, ...

Moving from One Part of the Presentation to Another

Now that I've explained . . . let me move on to . . . .
That, then, is the first advantage of . . . . Let's take a look at another important advantage.

Activity 10:   Using Transitions to Connect Ideas

1. Work individually. Imagine that you are giving a brief presentation using the following information. Write brief notes on index cards, using only key words to help you remember the information. Leave enough space on each note card to add transitional expressions as you plan your presentation.

    Ways of Coping with Stress

    I. Physical
       A. Exercise: jog, go bike riding, play tennis
       B. Eat regular, healthy meals: limit salt and sugar, control caffeine
       C. Avoid unhealthy habits: smoking, drinking alcohol, taking drugs
    II. Emotional
       A. Spend time with friends and family for emotional support and understanding
       B. Try to let go of bad feelings, anger
       C. Keep a positive outlook by looking at the good side of things
       D. Be ready to laugh at yourself and your mistakes

      III. Mental
         A. Control your thoughts. When you can't stop worrying, tell your-self, "Stop!"
         B. Ignore things that you can't control: traffic jams, flat tires, de-layed meetings, rude drivers
      IV. Mix of Physical, Emotional, Mental
         A. Get a pet
         B. Put variety in your life: take a trip, visit a new restaurant, go to the movies, find an interesting hobby, read a book, attend a cul-tural event

2. Plan a presentation using your note cards. Write the transitional expres-sions you plan to use on the appropriate note cards.
3. Now work with a partner. Take turns giving your presentations to each other using your notes. While one person is speaking, the partner should list all the transitional expressions the speaker uses.
4. When all the pairs have finished, one or two speakers may give their presentations to the class.

After you have planned the main points and supporting material, you have completed the body of your presentation. You are now ready to plan the other two parts of your presentation—the introduction and the conclusion.

Developing an Effective Introduction

The introduction to a presentation is especially important because listeners often decide in the first minute or two whether they want to pay attention to what you are going to say. The purpose of an introduction is to:

- Attract your listeners' interest
- Preview the content

Attracting Your Listeners' Interest

You need to think carefully about the first few sentences of your presenta-tion. How can you gain your listeners' interest? Here are several strategies:

1. Relate your topic to your listeners' concerns. Consider the audience analysis that you did earlier in this unit. What goals, problems, or expe-riences do your listeners have in common? To get their attention, you

might explain how you can help them achieve a goal, solve a problem, or improve their lives. What about their wants and needs? You might explain how you can help them make new friends, save money, or get better grades.

2. Tell an anecdote that relates to your topic. People seem to have a natural interest in hearing stories about people they know or have heard of.
3. Ask your listeners one or more questions. These questions will involve them and keep them interested in your presentation.
4. Use a quotation from an expert.
5. Offer an interesting or surprising fact, opinion, or statement.

Of course, your "attention grabber" must relate directly to your topic. In any case, try not to begin with, "The subject of my presentation is . . . ," or

"I'm going to talk to you about . . . ," since these are not interesting ways to start a presentation.

Previewing the Content

After getting your listeners' attention, you need to state your topic clearly and to preview the order of the main ideas. This preview will prepare the listeners for your presentation and help them follow your method of organization. Previewing the content also helps your listeners understand and remember the information.

In general, an effective introduction should be brief and to the point. You should never use the introduction to apologize to the audience for anything —for being nervous, for not being prepared, or for not being an expert on the subject. By taking a positive, confident approach from the beginning of your presentation, you will make the listeners eager to hear what you have to say on the subject.

DEVELOPING AN INTRODUCTION

Here are some sample introductions that attract attention and preview the content:

Relating Your Topic to Your Listeners' Concerns and Asking Questions

How many of you have flown across the ocean in the past year? How did you feel when you arrived at your destination? If you're like me, you felt tired, you couldn't think very clearly, and you had a lot of trouble sleeping for several days. These feelings are known as jet lag. Jet lag happens when you cross several time zones on a trip, and then you have to eat, sleep, and work at times when your body wants to do something else. Today I'm going to tell you how you can avoid jet lag by controlling four main factors—food, drink, activity, and light.

Telling an Anecdote

Yesterday evening, I took a bus home from work, as I usually do. I had had a good day at work, and was looking forward to a relaxing evening with my family. Well, the trip usually takes twenty minutes, but yesterday it took me more than an hour—all because of a traffic jam! By the time I got home, I was tired, hungry, and angry. And why was I in such a terrible mood? Because of traffic! This experience made me realize how traffic problems affect all of us. Today I'd like to talk to you about three ways of improving the traffic problem in our city. First, I'll talk about banning parking in the city; second, about banning cars from the center of town; and last, about improving public transportation.

Offering an Interesting Fact

I read an interesting fact in the newspaper yesterday: the average American teenager watches five to six hours of television every day. Can this much television be good for anyone? In my opinion, spending so much time in front of the television has many negative consequences. Today I'd like to focus on three consequences that I think are especially harmful. First, television encourages teenagers to waste their time. Second, television makes teenagers passive. And, finally, television gives teenagers a very unrealistic view of life.

Using a Quotation

In 1787 Thomas Jefferson said, and I quote, "Traveling. This makes men wiser, but less happy." I think if Jefferson were speaking today, he might say, "Traveling makes men *and women* wiser, but less happy." However, the message would be the same. Traveling certainly has its difficulties, but today I'd like to look at the ways it makes people wiser. I'll discuss three major benefits of traveling: first, educational benefits; then, cultural benefits; and finally, social benefits.

Activity 11:   Preparing an Introduction

1. Work with a partner. Consider the presentation on the disadvantages of living in the city discussed previously in this unit. Develop two introductions you might use in a four- to five-minute presentation on this topic. Each introduction should use a different method of attracting attention to your topic.

2. When all the pairs are ready, work in a large group or as a class. Pairs should take turns presenting their introductions (only the introduction —not the entire presentation). After each introduction, everyone should discuss:

   • What method was used to attract attention or gain interest?
   • Did the "attention grabber" clearly relate to or lead into the topic?
   • Did the introduction preview the content?

3. After all the pairs have presented their introductions, discuss which were the most effective. Why?

Developing a Strong Conclusion

The conclusion of your presentation is important because you want to leave a strong impression on your listeners. You should be brief and to the point in concluding your presentation. You don't want to surprise people by suddenly announcing, "That's all," or "I guess I'm finished." That kind of ending shows that you have not organized your ideas very well. Generally, in your conclusion, you want to:

- Signal that you are about to finish the presentation
- Make concluding comments
- Thank the audience
- Ask whether the listeners have any questions

You can use one of the following strategies in your concluding comments:

1. Summarize or review the main points you have presented.
2. Remind listeners of the importance of what you have said.
3. Predict future consequences of what you have described.
4. Ask your listeners to take appropriate action.

DEVELOPING A CONCLUSION

Signaling the Conclusion

In $\left\{ \begin{array}{l} \text{conclusion,} \\ \text{summary,} \end{array} \right\}$ . . . .

To $\left\{ \begin{array}{l} \text{summarize,} \\ \text{conclude,} \end{array} \right\}$ . . . .

Before I end, let me say . . . .

Asking for Questions

Do you have any questions or comments?
I'll be happy to answer any questions you may have.

Sample Conclusions

In conclusion, then, the consequences of television that I've mentioned are just too harmful to ignore. Teenagers need to get away from television and out into the real world. Instead of sitting in front of a black box, they should be meeting people, playing sports, doing homework, and developing their talents. Thank you. Do you have any questions or comments?

Before I end, let me summarize the main points I've mentioned. The next time you're getting ready to travel overseas, just remember — food, drink, activity, and light. By following the suggestions I've given you regarding these four factors, you should be able to avoid jet lag completely. Thank you. I'll be happy to answer any questions you have.

Activity 12:   Preparing a Conclusion

1. Work with a partner. Consider the presentation on the disadvantages of living in the city discussed previously in this unit. Develop a conclusion that you might use in a four- to five-minute presentation on this topic.
2. When all the pairs are ready, work in a large group or as a class. Pairs should take turns presenting their conclusions (only the conclusion—not the entire presentation).
3. After all the pairs have presented their conclusions, discuss which were the most effective. Why?

Activity 13:   Selecting a Topic for a Presentation

1. Work individually. Choose several topics that you could use for a four-
   to five-minute presentation. (You can find a list of possible subjects in
   Appendix B.) Be sure to narrow your subject to a topic, consider your audience analysis, and keep the time limit in mind as you think of possible
   topics. List five possible topics below:

   A. _____

   B. _____

   C. _____

   D. _____

   E. _____

2. When everyone has finished, work in a small group. Take turns presenting your ideas for topics to the group. Group members should try to
   help each speaker choose three topics that are the most interesting to the
   group. During the discussion, you may want to change the wording of
   your topics or even add new ones.
3. When all the groups have finished, each person should give the teacher a
   list of three topics for a presentation. Your teacher will then be able to
   help you choose the best topic for a class presentation.

Activity 14:   Developing a Presentation

1. Work individually. Using the topic you selected in Activity 13, plan a
   four- to five-minute class presentation. Start developing your presentation by following the guidelines in Appendix C. Pay careful attention to
   organizing your ideas, using transitions, and developing an effective introduction and conclusion.
2. When everyone has finished, work in pairs. Take turns practicing your
   presentations, making sure that they meet the time limit.
3. Give your presentation to a group or to the class. You may use notes, but
   do not read or memorize your presentation.
4. Observers or your teacher may use the Presentation Evaluation II Form
   in Appendix A.

Pronunciation Practice

Rhythm and Reductions

As mentioned in Unit 4, the rhythm of spoken English results from the alternation of stressed and unstressed syllables. The contrast between stressed and unstressed syllables is made even stronger by the way speakers reduce (or weaken) unstressed syllables or words within a sentence. In fact, in natural, spoken English, unstressed syllables and words become even more reduced as speech gets faster.

Unstressed words of one syllable are some of the most frequently used words in English: *a, an, the, of, or, and, for,* and *to.* Thus, it is important to understand how these words sound when used in phrases or sentences.

Activity 15:   Listening to Unstressed Words in Sentences

Listen to Activity 15 on the tape. Listen to the way the unstressed words are pronounced in each sentence. Repeat each sentence after the speaker.

Stressed Form	**Unstressed Form**
1. *a*	They're in *a* hurry.
	I'll be there in *a* minute.
	That's not *a* problem.
	Mary's *a* teacher.
2. *an*	We'll leave in *an* hour.
	I have *an* idea.
	He's *an* engineer.
	It was *an* interesting discussion.
3. *the*	What's *the* problem?
	Room 204 is on *the* right.
	Their books are under *the* table.
	Stand in front of *the* class.
4. *of*	I talked to a lot *of* people.
	I'd like a copy *of* the report.
	She's one *of* the best managers here.
	I have a different point *of* view.
5. *or*	You can come by bus *or* subway.
	She spoke for five *or* six minutes.
	We walked three *or* four blocks.
	Take one *or* two deep breaths.

6. *and*   Bob *and* Jane were late.
              Speak clearly *and* slowly.
              Try to arrive between one *and* one-thirty.
              Keep your comments *and* questions brief.

7. *for*   I sat there *for* an hour.
              He did it *for* free.
              They're ready *for* the test.
              That's enough *for* now.

8. *to*   They have a right *to* privacy.
              She'd like *to* talk *to* you.
              I need *to* see the manager.
              We'll be there from three *to* four.

You may sometimes have difficulty hearing the difference between *is/isn't, are/aren't, was/wasn't, were/weren't, has/hasn't, have/haven't, can/can't,* and *should/shouldn't.* If you have this problem, pay attention to whether the word is stressed or unstressed in the sentence. In the affirmative, these function words are unstressed (unless they come at the end of a sentence). However, in the negative, these words are stressed since they express meaning in the sentence.

Activity 16:   Listening for Differences

Listen to Activity 16 on the tape. The speaker will say each sentence twice. Pay attention to whether the words are stressed or unstressed.

1. **A.** Pat *is* here.
   B. Pat *isn't* here.
2. **A.** Those people *are* paying attention.
   B. Those people *aren't* paying attention.
3. **A.** Mary *was* upset with her boss.
   B. Mary *wasn't* upset with her boss.
4. **A.** The speakers *were* well-organized.
   B. The speakers *weren't* well-organized.
5. **A.** Carol *has* studied French.
   B. Carol *hasn't* studied French.
6. **A.** The students *have* worked hard.
   B. The students *haven't* worked hard.

7. **A.** You *can* take a break now.
   B. You *can't* take a break now.
8. **A.** Ron *should* speak to his boss about that.
   B. Ron *shouldn't* speak to his boss about that.

Activity 17:   Listening to Stressed and Unstressed Forms

Listen to Activity 17 on the tape. Notice the way the affirmative form is stressed at the end of the sentence, but unstressed within the sentence. Repeat each sentence or question after the speaker.

1. **A.** Can we leave now?
   B. I'm not sure if we can.
   C. We can leave in a few minutes.

2. **A.** Is Tom absent?
   B. I don't know if he is.
   C. I think he's coming late.

3. **A.** Were the students angry?
   B. I think they were.
   C. No, I think they were tired.

4. **A.** Are the books expensive?
   B. Yes, they are.
   C. It seems to me they're reasonable.

5. **A.** Have your friends left yet?
   B. I believe they have.
   C. Yes, they've left.

Activity 18:   Identifying Affirmative and Negative Statements

Listen to Activity 18 on the tape. The speaker will say each sentence twice. In the following blanks, write *A* if the statement is affirmative or *N* if the statement is negative.

1. _____   5. _____   9. _____

2. _____   6. _____   10. _____

3. _____   7. _____   11. _____

4. _____   8. _____   12. _____

Learning Strategies

Considering Successful Language Learners

Experts have identified a number of characteristics that are typical of successful language learners. These characteristics are listed in the chart in Activity 19. Which of these apply to you?

Activity 19: Analyzing Your Language Learning Characteristics

1. Work individually. Consider the way you are learning English. Use the following key to indicate how often the following statements apply to you:

   3 = frequently   2 = sometimes   1 = seldom/never

WHEN LEARNING ENGLISH, YOU. . . .	POINTS
A. Try to answer even if you are not sure of the answer	
B. Are willing to make mistakes, take chances, and take risks	
C. Accept that not all language rules "make sense" or are logical	
D. Try to find patterns in the language	
E. Make an effort to find opportunities to practice the language	
F. Use many ways to communicate when speaking, such as gesturing, drawing pictures, and "talking around" unknown words	
G. Try to learn from your own and others' mistakes, not always depending on the teacher for correction	
H. Try to relate new information to what you have learned	
I. Speak to native speakers as much as possible	
J. Try to guess the meanings of new or unknown words	
K. Speak silently to yourself in English as you are walking, sitting, riding the bus, etc.	
L. Answer all questions mentally in class	

WHEN LEARNING ENGLISH, YOU. . . .	POINTS
M. Use new words and structures as much as possible in speaking and writing	
N. Keep on trying, even if a task seems difficult	
O. Try to think in English as you are speaking or reading, without translating everything mentally	
TOTAL POINTS	

2. After you have added your total points, analyze your score according to the scale:

38–45: Excellent! You seem to have the characteristics of a successful language learner. Keep up the good work!

23–37: Good. Try to practice the skills or strategies in which you scored 1 or 2 points. In this way, you can be an even better language learner!

15–22: You should analyze the way you are studying English. Are you making the best use of your time and energy? Try to work on developing the skills or strategies in which you scored 1 or 2 points. If necessary, get some advice from your teacher.

3. When everyone has finished, work as a class. Discuss the following:

- Do you think these characteristics are "inborn," or can you work at developing them?
- Which of the characteristics listed in the chart seem to be the most difficult to achieve?

Cross-Cultural Communication

Considering Classroom Behavior

Classroom behavior is different in different cultures.

Activity 20: Comparing Behavior

1. Work individually. On the following questionnaire, write what you know about your own culture and what you think is usual in American culture. Do not limit yourself to the given examples. Feel free to use your own ideas.

IN YOUR CULTURE	SITUATIONS	IN AMERICAN CULTURE
	A. If you have a serious problem with the way the teacher is conducting class, to whom do you speak? • Another teacher • The director • Other students • No one • The teacher	
	B. Your teacher gave you a much lower grade for a class presentation than you expected. What do you do? • Do nothing. Work harder on your next presentation. • Complain to someone in authority. • During class, ask the teacher to explain your grade. • Make an appointment to speak with your teacher outside of class.	

IN YOUR CULTURE	SITUATIONS	IN AMERICAN CULTURE
	C. You have a five-minute presentation due today. Late last night, you realized that you do not have enough to say. Your presentation will probably take only two minutes or so. What do you do? • Give the presentation, but first explain that it will be short. • Do the best you can, without making excuses. • When the teacher calls on you to give your presentation, ask if you can give it another day. • Explain your situation to the teacher before class and ask for a postponement.	
	D. You need a letter of recommendation from your English teacher. You go to see her during office hours. What do you do? • Spend fifteen minutes in polite conversation before you explain your situation and ask her to write the letter. • After exchanging greetings for a minute or two, explain your situation and ask her to write the letter. • During a general conversation, mention that you need a letter of recommendation, but do not directly ask her to write it.	

2. When everyone has finished, share your answers as a class.
3. Turn to the Answer Key on page 221 to see some typical responses of people in the United States.

Unit 6

Taking a Stand

- Describe the scene in the photograph.
- What are the possible consequences—both positive and negative—of allowing women in combat?
- Should the military allow women in combat? Why or why not?

Listening Practice

Activity 1:   Considering Consequences

1. Work in a small group. Before doing this activity, you may want to read the box "Examining Consequences" in this unit. Consider the following situation. Then use a separate sheet of paper to list as many ideas as you can in response to the discussion question.

   Situation. Twenty-four years ago, a young man received a prison sentence of twenty years to life for murdering a famous rock-and-roll singer. Since that time, the killer has avoided making any public statements from prison. Now, however, someone has written a book about the killer's life. The author explains that the killer murdered the rock star because he was jealous of the man's fame. A television station is planning to broadcast a special hour-long interview with this killer from prison.

   Discussion. What are the possible consequences of broadcasting this interview? (Be sure to consider the killer, the singer's family, the public, the author, etc.)

2. Now listen to Activity 1A on the tape. You will hear a man and a woman discussing the possible consequences of broadcasting the interview. How many consequences that they mention are the same as the ones you listed in item 1 above? Put a check on your paper next to those consequences.

3. Listen to Activity 1B on the tape. You will hear the same conversation broken into shorter segments. For each segment, write the consequence that the speakers are discussing.

Vocabulary

publicity = information that brings public attention to someone or something

A. _____

B. _____

C. _____

D. _____

E. _____

F. _____

G. _____

H. _____

I. _____

J. _____

4. Work in a group or as a class to compare your answers. Then, after discussing your ideas and the ideas discussed on the tape, decide whether the overall consequences of broadcasting the interview seem more beneficial or more harmful.

Activity 2: Getting Clarification

1. Work in a small group. Consider the following situation. Then use a separate sheet of paper to write your answers to the discussion questions.

   Situation. Several days ago a newspaper investigation revealed that in the past year local hospitals and clinics have treated at least twenty pilots for drug abuse. Approximately 90 percent of these cases involved cocaine overdoses. Doctors cannot report these pilots to the airlines, the police, or aviation authorities because of these patients' right to confidentiality.

   Discussion
   • What rights and/or obligations do pilots have in this situation?
   • What rights and/or obligations do doctors have?
   • What are the possible consequences of keeping this information confidential?
   • What are the possible consequences of reporting pilots who are getting treatment for drug abuse to authorities?

2. Listen to Activity 2 on the tape. You will hear several segments of a conversation related to the situation. In each segment, one of the speakers is asking for clarification. Write the expression each speaker uses to ask for clarification.

   A. _____

   B. _____

   C. _____

   D. _____

   E. _____

   F. _____

3. Listen to Activity 2 on the tape again. This time listen to the opinions presented by the first speaker in each segment. What point is each speaker trying to make? Write this idea in your own words.

A. The man thinks _____

_____

B. The woman thinks _____

_____

C. The man thinks _____

_____

D. The woman thinks _____

_____

E. The man thinks _____

_____

F. The woman thinks _____

_____

4. Work in a group or as a class to compare your answers.

Communication Skills

In Unit 4, we examined controversial issues by considering the rights, obligations, and values involved. In this unit, we will consider the possible consequences of an action or decision. First, though, we will consider the responsibilities of the leader of a discussion group.

Leading a Group Discussion

Group leaders generally have the responsibility of making sure that a discussion is fair and polite. As a group leader, you need to:

1. Start and conclude the activity, paying attention to the time limits.
2. Make sure that all group members have an equal chance to participate. You may need to control people who talk too much and to involve quiet members.

3. Keep the discussion on the subject. If participants move onto a completely different subject or start bringing up irrelevant points, you should politely bring the discussion back to the subject.

4. Keep the discussion moving. You may have to cut off conversation politely if members spend too much time on one point or start repeating the same ideas. However, you also have to decide when conversation is useful and should be encouraged.

5. Make sure that all group members can understand each other. You may have to ask people to speak more slowly or more loudly so that everyone can understand them. You may also have to help speakers who are having difficulties explaining their ideas.

6. Summarize when needed and look for areas of agreement. Make sure that all participants understand and accept the group decision.

The following box includes some expressions that a group leader might use during a discussion:

LEADING A DISCUSSION

Getting Started

Okay, are we ready to get started?
Is everyone ready to begin?

Encouraging Everyone to Participate

So, who would like to comment on what John said?
What do you think about Mary's point?
Does anyone have anything to add?

Bringing People into the Discussion

John, what do you $\begin{cases} \text{think?} \\ \text{suggest?} \end{cases}$
Mary, do you have anything to add?

Controlling People Who Talk Too Much

Let's hear what some others have to say.
I think you've got a good point there. Why don't we find out what some others think about this?

Clarifying

I'm not sure we all understand what you mean.
I'm afraid we don't really understand what you said.
Could you explain that again?

Keeping the Discussion on the Subject

Yes, that's an interesting idea, but it raises a different point. Could we come back to that a little later?
That's an interesting idea, but isn't that a different point? Perhaps we should finish this point before going on.

Keeping the Discussion Moving

Perhaps we should go on to the next point.
We have only five minutes left, so we'd better move on.
Are there any more comments before we move on to the next point?

Reaching Agreement and Summing Up

Do we agree that . . . ?
So, to sum up, we've decided . . . .

Activity 3:   Reviewing Useful Expressions

1. Work with a partner. Review the expressions listed in the box "Leading a Discussion." Without looking at the list, write what the leader can say when the following situations occur during a discussion:

    A. Tim, a group member, starts talking about a different topic.

    _____

    B. Jack, a shy student, has not said anything for the past fifteen minutes.

    _____

    C. Sue is speaking so fast that no one can understand her.

    _____

    D. Kathleen is speaking so softly that no one can hear her.

    _____

    E. Bill has been explaining an idea for more than two minutes without letting anyone else say anything.

    _____

    F. Grace has just finished explaining an idea, but no one seems to understand what she is talking about.

    _____

    G. Before the discussion starts, all the group members are making small talk and do not seem ready to begin.

    _____

    H. Several group members have been discussing a point for a long time and keep repeating the same ideas.

    _____

    I. After five minutes of a discussion, everyone stops talking. No one seems to have anything to say.

    _____

    J. Everyone must leave in two minutes, so it is time to end the discussion.

    _____

2. When all the pairs have finished, compare your answers as a class.

Examining Consequences

Consequences are the effects, either beneficial or harmful, that an action or decision may have. As you consider consequences, be sure to think of all the people or groups that may be affected by a particular action or decision. Furthermore, try to look at an action from many points of view to see what consequences it might have. In trying to think of different consequences, remember the categories for grouping main ideas mentioned in Unit 5. These same categories can be applied to types of consequences:

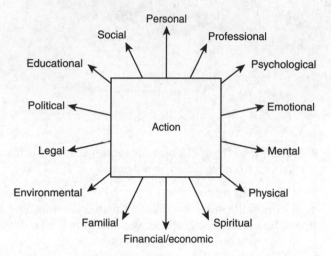

Considering a Specific Example

Let's examine a decision by considering its possible consequences:

> *Situation.* George Wilson has spent all evening in a bar with one of his colleagues, Tom Stewart. When it's time for the bar to close, George is very drunk. Tom says they should call a cab to take them home. George, however, insists that he wants to drive himself home. The drive takes about fifteen minutes, and George says he will be okay. Tom decides he cannot stop George from driving home alone.

> *Discussion*

A. Who might be affected by Tom's decision?

- Tom
- George
- George's family
- Other drivers on the road and their passengers
- Pedestrians

B. What are the possible consequences of Tom's decision to allow George to drive when he's drunk?

- Tom will worry.
- Tom will probably feel responsible if something happens to George.
- The police may stop George and give him a ticket.
- George could kill or injure others.
- George may kill or injure himself.
- George might damage his car or another car.
- George may get home with no problems.
- George's family might be angry that Tom allowed him to drive home drunk.

Group Decision. In this situation, most people would agree that the possible harmful consequences are so severe that they carry more weight than any possible beneficial consequences. Therefore, Tom should *not* allow George to drive home.

DISCUSSING CONSEQUENCES

Speakers can use one of two grammatical structures to discuss future consequences. The basic difference between them is the speaker's attitude.

Real Conditionals

Speakers use this form if they feel that a particular action is likely to occur. In the following sentences, the speaker seems to think that George will probably drive home.

Definite Consequences

If George *drives* home, Tom *will worry*.

Possible Consequences

If George drives home, he $\begin{Bmatrix} might \\ may \\ could \end{Bmatrix}$ *have* an accident.

Hypothetical (Unreal) Conditionals

Speakers use this form if they feel uncertain or unsure that a particular action will occur. They may be discussing many possible actions, or they may be imagining the consequences of each. In the following sentences, the speaker isn't sure whether George is going to drive home.

Definite Consequences

If George *drove* home, Tom *would worry*.

Possible Consequences

If George drove home, he $\begin{Bmatrix} might \\ may \\ could \end{Bmatrix}$ *have* an accident.

In most situations, there is not a right or a wrong conditional to use. One speaker might use the real conditional if he or she feels that this action is a definite possibility. Another speaker, however, may not feel so sure about the same action.

Looking at a Chain of Possible Consequences

In considering consequences, you may also see a chain of possible effects resulting from a certain action or decision. That is, if one thing happens, then another thing might happen, then another, and so forth. Consider a chain of possible consequences that might result from Tom's decision not to stop George from driving home drunk: George might kill someone in an accident.

- If George kills someone, the police will probably arrest him.
- If the police arrest him, he might have to stand trial.
- If he stands trial, the jury might find him guilty.
- If the jury finds him guilty, he may go to jail.
- If he goes to jail, his life will be ruined.
- If his life is ruined, he might blame Tom for not stopping him.

Activity 4:   Considering a Chain of Possible Consequences

1. Work in a small group. Consider the following situation:

   Situation. Elizabeth is a good student. She has an important exam in chemistry today, but didn't have time to study for it last night. She has written all the important formulas on a very small piece of paper that she plans to use during the exam. She knows this is cheating, but she feels she has no other choice.

2. Work together to develop a chain of possible consequences if the teacher catches Elizabeth cheating.

   A. If the teacher catches Elizabeth cheating, _____

   _____

   B. If _____

   _____

   C. If _____

   _____

   D. If _____

   _____

3. When all the groups have finished, share your ideas as a class.

Activity 5:   Considering Possible Consequences

1. Work in a small group. Consider the following situations. Use a separate sheet of paper to write your answers to these questions:

   • Who might be affected by each action?
   • What are the possible consequences of the action?

   A. *Situation.* The professors at this university are planning to stop giving exams completely—no quizzes, chapter tests, midterm exams, or final exams.

   B. *Situation.* Nurses are very upset about their low pay and poor working conditions in public hospitals throughout the city. City officials have refused their request for a pay raise. They say that the city cannot afford raises for at least the next year. Nurses have voted to go on strike.

C. *Situation.* Executives at a large automobile factory are concerned about workers who are wasting a lot of time on the job. Factory officials say that these workers are standing around and talking with their friends instead of working. Therefore, the officials are planning to install video cameras around the factory to enable them to watch these workers at all times.

2. When all the groups have finished, share your ideas as a class. For each situation, decide whether the possible consequences are more beneficial than harmful, or more harmful than beneficial.

Listening Actively

As you may know, people in a group discussion can become quite frustrated if they feel that others are not listening to their ideas. Furthermore, when people are more interested in speaking than in listening, communication can break down completely. Therefore, effective listening is an essential skill in a discussion.

Activity 6: Focusing on Listening Habits

1. Work individually. Answer the following questions:

   A. Think of times you have been speaking to someone who is not listening to you. What do such people do to show you that they are not listening?

   _____

   _____

   _____

   B. Think of people you know who are good listeners. What do these people do to let you know that they are really listening to you?

   _____

   _____

   _____

2. Work in a small group or as a class to share your answers.

Many people have poor listening habits. For example, some people think about what they are going to say next rather than listening to what the speaker is saying. Others listen only to what interests them and do not bother to pay attention to anything else. You can improve your listening skills by following these guidelines:

1. Give the speaker all of your attention. Do not look through papers, read notes, or draw pictures while the person is speaking.
2. Use suitable body language to make it clear that you are paying attention—look directly at people when they are speaking, smile sometimes, and nod when you agree with what they have said.
3. Examine the speaker's ideas by asking questions and getting further information. Do not rush to discuss your own ideas or change the subject. Be sure to ask for clarification if you do not understand what the speaker has said.
4. If you disagree with what the other person is saying, try to get a full understanding of that point of view before you speak. It often helps to re-

state or paraphrase the other person's idea to make sure that you have understood it correctly.

5. Be patient. Let the speaker finish before you begin to speak. If you interrupt, the speaker may feel that you are not interested in what he or she has to say.

6. If the speaker is making a point that you disagree with, do *not* plan what you are going to say while he or she is still talking. If you are trying to think of what to say, you cannot pay attention to the speaker's message.

LISTENING ACTIVELY

Asking for Clarification

What do you mean?
I'm not sure what you mean.
Sorry, but I don't understand what you mean.
Could you explain what you mean by . . . ?
Are you saying that . . . ?
I'm not sure I follow you. Did you say that . . . ?

Clarifying or Restating

I mean . . . .
In other words, ...
The point I'm trying to make is . . . .

Paraphrasing

John said that . . . .
What Mary means is . . . .
I believe Dan's point is . . . .
I think Anne feels . . . . Isn't that right?
Let me see if I understood. You said . . . .

Checking for Understanding

Do you see what I mean?
Is that clear?

Activity 7:   Practicing Active Listening

1. Work in a small group. Consider the following situation. Members of your group should take the positions of the different participants in the discussion.

Situation. The head of security at BANT Airlines received a frightening phone call this morning. The caller warned the security director that a bomb would be placed aboard a plane flying between the United States and Europe sometime within the next week. Police officials have determined that this is an extremely serious threat and not a joke. Of course, the company has taken immediate steps to increase security. The head of security wants to make this bomb threat public. The managing director of the airlines, however, feels that it is necessary to keep it a secret from the public. The president of the company has called an emergency meeting.

Special Guidelines. For the first ten minutes of the group discussion, everyone who speaks must begin by restating or paraphrasing what the previous speaker has said. The previous speaker has to nod his or her head to indicate whether this paraphrasing is correct. The new speaker may not continue until he or she has correctly restated what the person has said. After ten minutes, you may then continue the discussion without following the rule, but be sure to continue listening carefully to each speaker.

Participants
President of the company
Managing director
Head of BANT security operations

Group Decision. What action, if any, should airline officials take in this situation?

_____

_____

_____

Reasons

_____

_____

_____

_____

2. At the end of the discussion, consider the following:

- How did the special guidelines affect the discussion?
- How difficult was this type of practice?
- Was it more difficult for some people than others?

- Do you feel that it's important for speakers to refer to what previous speakers have said? Why or why not?

3. After all the groups have finished, compare your ideas as a class.

Judging Ethical Behavior

In examining controversial issues, you often need to think about your moral principles—that is, your ideas of right and wrong. A term frequently used in relation to moral principles is *ethics*. The term *ethical* describes actions or decisions that you believe are good or right in a particular situation.

Many activities in this unit involve ethical dilemmas. An ethical dilemma is a situation in which you need to choose between two or more possible actions or solutions that involve conflicting rights, obligations, and values. For example, imagine you have just discovered that a good friend is stealing money from the office where you both work. This situation requires you to consider a number of conflicts, such as loyalty to your friend versus loyalty to your employer, and compassion versus honesty. In addition, you need to consider the possible consequences—both beneficial and harmful—of each action you might take in this situation.

Other types of ethical dilemmas may require you to decide which is more important:

- a person's right to privacy or the public's right to know
- a person's obligation to maintain confidentiality or that person's obligation to protect public safety
- compassion or fairness

These dilemmas are not clear-cut cases of right versus wrong or good versus evil. This means that in dealing with an ethical dilemma, you need to examine the specific facts and special circumstances of the situation. As you focus on the situation, you can begin to identify the rights, obligations, values, and/or possible consequences involved. You may find that several of these considerations seem to be in conflict, yet also seem to be equally important. You then have to decide which of these considerations is the most important or has the highest priority *in this particular situation*. After determining all the possible actions you might take, you can select the option that best reflects the most important consideration(s). This type of reasoning allows you to choose the course of action that you believe is the most ethical—even if none of the options seems completely right.

In solving an ethical dilemma, you may be guided by some general principles that combine important rights, obligations, values, and consequences:

1. As far as possible, follow the "Golden Rule": Do unto others as you would have them do unto you. In other words, you should treat other people the way you want them to treat you.
2. The chosen course of action should accomplish the greatest good or cause the least harm.
3. The chosen action should accomplish the greatest good for the greatest number of people.

STATING PRIORITIES

In my opinion, the main thing is . . . .
As I see it, the most important point is . . . .
I feel that the most important consideration is . . . .
I believe that the highest priority here is . . . .

Activity 8:   Considering an Ethical Issue

1. Work as a class. Consider the following situation:

   Situation.   A newspaper reporter has recently learned that a world-famous professional basketball player, Mike Ellis, is HIV positive. That is, he is carrying the virus that causes AIDS. After checking carefully, the reporter finds out that the twenty-five-year-old athlete tested positive for the virus about a year ago. However, Mike has managed to keep this information a secret from the public. When the reporter calls the athlete to get further information, Mike sounds very upset and says, "Please don't publish this story. You will ruin my life!" The reporter knows that Mike has a wife and young child, but he decides to publish the story in the newspaper anyway.

2. Work individually. Consider both of the following points of view, adding any other reasons you can think of. Then put a check in front of the letter of the position that you personally feel has the strongest arguments.

   _____ **A.** Yes, publishing the story revealing that Mike Ellis is HIV positive *is ethical* because:

- The public has a right to know.
- The reporter has a professional obligation to publish an important story on a public figure.
- Mike's teammates and opponents have a right to know that he is HIV positive.
- Because Mike is a popular athlete, more people might feel sympathy for others who are HIV positive or who have AIDS.
- Mike might be able to persuade people to change their behavior so they are not at risk of contracting the disease.

_____ **B.** No, publishing the story *isn't* ethical because:

- The athlete has a right to privacy.
- Publishing the story isn't compassionate.
- The article may ruin Mike's life.
- Mike will probably lose his job.
- His wife and child will suffer from the negative publicity.
- Mike might lose some friends.

3. Now work in a small group to reach agreement on the following question:

Group Decision. Is it ethical for the reporter to publish the story revealing that Mike Ellis is HIV positive?

_____ Yes   _____ No

4. When all the groups have finished, share your ideas as a class.

Activity 9:   Examining an Ethical Issue

1. Work in a small group. Consider the following situation, developing reasons to support *both* points of view. Then work together to decide which position, A or B, has the strongest arguments. That is, which position seems to be more beneficial than harmful overall? If both are harmful, choose the one that seems the *least* harmful.

   Situation. Susan Barrows is a physician working in the emergency room. She is treating a sixteen-year-old high school student, Janice Young, who has suffered minor injuries in a car accident. During the physical examination, Dr. Barrows finds out that Janice is three-months pregnant. Janice says she has not gone to a doctor because she does not want anyone to find out she is pregnant. Janice absolutely refuses to tell her parents that she is pregnant. Her parents are in the waiting room.

   Considering Both Sides of the Issue
   A. It *is* ethical for Dr. Barrows to inform Janice's parents that she is pregnant because:

   _____

   _____

   _____

   _____

   B. It *isn't* ethical for Dr. Barrows to inform Janice's parents that she is pregnant because:

   _____

   _____

   _____

   _____

Group Decision. As a group, do you believe it is ethical for Dr. Barrows to inform Janice's parents that she is pregnant?

_____ Yes   _____ No

2. When all the groups have finished, share your ideas as a class.

Activity 10:   Judging Ethical Conduct

1. Work in a small group. Discuss the following situations in order to bring out any rights, obligations, values, or consequences that might be involved. Then work together to reach agreement on a group decision. Write the strongest reason(s) for arriving at this decision. After discussing each situation, fill in the observation form in Activity 11.

   A. *Situation.* Ralph Broderick believes that his wife, Sally, has started seeing another man romantically. Sally has told him that there is no one else in her life, but Ralph does not believe her. In fact, Ralph's fears and distrust of Sally are ruining their relationship. Finally, to discover the truth, Ralph hides a device in the telephone that allows him to make secret recordings of calls to and from his home.

   Group Decision. Is it ethical for Ralph to make secret recordings of telephone calls to and from his home?

   _____ Yes   _____ No

   Reasons

   _____

   _____

   B. *Situation.* Jane Smith is an Olympic athlete who competes in long-distance running. In the last Olympics, she was very upset when she lost an important race. In the news conference after the race, Jane said that she believed the winner had used illegal drugs to improve her performance. In fact, Jane believes that a number of athletes are using illegal drugs. When reporters asked her for evidence, she said, "I don't have any definite proof, but I have a right to state my personal opinion."

   Group Decision. Is it ethical for Jane to make this statement to reporters?

   _____ Yes   _____ No

Reasons

_____

_____

C. *Situation.* Helen Stokes left work yesterday at 5:00. When she was about a block from her house, she saw several police cars parked in her driveway. In a panic, she raced down the street, jumped out of her car, and ran toward the house. A police officer stopped her from entering the house. He explained that someone had just killed her husband and two children. As Mrs. Stokes started screaming hysterically, a newspaper photographer took several pictures of her. The editor of the newspaper is planning to put one of these photographs of her along with the article on the murders in tomorrow's newspaper.

Group Decision. Is it ethical for the newspaper to print this photograph of Mrs. Stokes?

_____ Yes _____ No

Reasons

_____

_____

D. *Situation.* Last week Dr. Price informed a patient, Frank Walker, that he is HIV positive. Frank was very upset and insisted that the doctor keep this information completely confidential. The doctor, of course, told Frank that he had to tell his wife immediately. In fact, Frank and his wife have recently separated and are planning to get a divorce. Frank is afraid that his wife will use this information against him in court. His biggest fear is that he will lose custody of his children. Frank, therefore, refuses to tell his wife. In this state, the law requires a doctor to get written permission from the patient before giving the results of an HIV test to anyone else.

Group Decision. Is it ethical for Dr. Price to inform Frank's wife about the HIV test results?

_____ Yes _____ No

Reasons

_____

_____

2. When all the groups have finished, share your ideas as a class.

Activity 11:   Evaluating Your Participation

1. Work individually. After discussing each situation in Activity 10, use the following key to answer the questions in the chart:

+ = yes   √ = partially   − = no

QUESTIONS	SITUATION A	SITUATION B	SITUATION C	SITUATION D
A. Are you presenting your ideas?				
B. Are you supporting your ideas with reasons?				
C. Are you asking others for their ideas?				
D. Is everyone participating?				
E. Are you listening actively?				

2. After everyone has finished, compare your results as a class. Then discuss the following:

- Did group participation improve as you moved from situation to situation?
- In general, did everyone in your group participate equally?

Supporting a Position

In many social, academic, and professional situations, you will be asked whether or not you agree with particular actions or decisions. In supporting your point of view, you can consider rights, obligations, values, and consequences.

Activity 12: Considering Opposing Points of View

1. Work in a small group. Consider the following situations, developing reasons to support *both* points of view. Then work together to reach agreement on a group decision. In your discussion, be sure to consider rights, obligations, values, and consequences.

   A. *Situation.* It is a tradition at City High School in the United States that the senior with the highest grade point average gives the farewell speech at graduation ceremonies. In February of this year, school officials notified Patricia Moreland that she would be the graduation speaker in June. Last week, however, two months before the ceremony, Patricia admitted that she is four-months pregnant and has no plans to get married. School officials are planning to replace Patricia with another speaker.

   Discussion. Should school officials allow Patricia to give the graduation speech?

   Reasons for

   _____

   _____

   _____

Reasons against

_____

_____

_____

Group Decision. What should school officials do?

_____

_____

_____

B. *Situation.* Most news organizations have a policy of not revealing the identities of rape victims. However, a newspaper is planning to publish the name and picture of a twenty-five-year-old woman who says she was raped by a well-known politician. The trial of this case is just beginning and has attracted a lot of public attention. The name and photograph of the politician have appeared in newspapers and magazines around the country.

Discussion. Should the newspaper reveal the identity of the rape victim?

Reasons for

_____

_____

_____

Reasons against

_____

_____

_____

Group Decision. What should the editor of the newspaper do?

_____

_____

2. When all the groups have finished, share your ideas as a class.

Activity 13:   Taking a Stand

1. Work in a small group. Consider the following situations. Work together to reach agreement on a group decision. Write the strongest reasons for arriving at this decision. The teacher or observers may use the Individual Evaluation of Group Members Form in Appendix A.

   A. *Situation.* A journalist is writing an article about a well-known American politician. This politician publicly opposes the gay and lesbian movement in the United States. The journalist, however, has definite proof that the politician's son is secretly gay.

   Group Decision. Should the journalist include the information that the politician's son is gay in the article?

   _____ Yes   _____ No

   Reasons

   _____

   _____

   B. *Situation.* A twenty-seven-year-old divorced mother, Jane Lawson, has legal custody of her two children, ages five and seven. One afternoon last week she left them alone at home for two hours. The problem was that she had an emergency at work and she couldn't find a babysitter to stay with the children. Ms. Lawson says that the children were safe because she made sure all the windows and doors were locked. The children's father, who stopped by the house by chance, found the children alone and reported the incident to police. The father is now trying to get custody of the children.

   Group Decision. Should Ms. Lawson lose custody of her children because of this incident?

   _____ Yes   _____ No

   Reasons

   _____

   _____

2. When all the groups have finished, share your ideas as a class.

Pronunciation Practice

Linking within Thought Groups

English speakers usually show the relationship between ideas by grouping related words into phrases. These phrases are called thought groups. Examples of typical thought groups are:

- nouns + modifiers: *a long meeting, some good managers*
- auxiliary verbs + main verb: *are going to have, should have done*
- preposition + object: *in the office, to the boss*
- adverbs + adjective: *very good, quite angry*
- pronoun subjects + verbs: *she left, he stopped*
- introductory expressions: *in my opinion, it seems to me*

When speaking, people may pause briefly between thought groups to make the meaning clear, to emphasize an idea, or simply to take a breath. An important note here is that brief pauses *between* thought groups are natural, but pauses *within* a thought group can cause confusion for your listeners.

The words within a thought group are not pronounced as separate units. They are pronounced smoothly, in one breath, without stopping after each word. Often, one word within a thought group seems to blend into the next. This happens because speakers often link the final sound of one word with the initial sound of the next. This linking of sounds can make it more difficult for learners of English to understand the spoken language.

Activity 14:   Linking with Vowels

Listen to Activity 14 on the tape. Listen to the speaker pronounce the following two word verbs. Notice the way the speaker moves the final consonant sound of the first word over to join the initial vowel sound of the following word. Repeat the words and then each sentence after the speaker.

1. turn on   Please turn on the lights.
2. get off   Let's get off the bus.
3. take off   Please take off your coat.
4. put away   Put away your books.
5. look into   We have to look into the problem.

6. find out   It's time to find out the truth.
7. make up   You can't make up the test.
8. give up   Don't give up yet.

Activity 15:   Listening to Linking in Past Tense Verbs

Listen to Activity 15 on the tape. Notice how the speaker links the past tense ending to the initial vowel sound of the next word. Repeat each sentence after the speaker.

1. The students showed us the campus.
2. We lived in Los Angeles.
3. I called up my friend.
4. Several companies closed at noon.
5. They finished at six o'clock.
6. We turned up the radio.

Activity 16:   Identifying Past Tense Verbs

Listen to Activity 16 on the tape. In each item the speaker will say the same sentence twice. Put a check in front of the sentence you hear.

1. _____ A. Those stores open at ten.

   _____ B. Those stores opened at ten.

2. _____ A. They walk into class late.

   _____ B. They walked into class late.

3. _____ A. People laugh at the teacher's jokes.

   _____ B. People laughed at the teacher's jokes.

4. _____ A. We complain about poor service.

   _____ B. We complained about poor service.

5. _____ A. I talk about my boss.

   _____ B. I talked about my boss.

6. _____ **A.** We study English grammar.

   _____ **B.** We studied English grammar.

7. _____ **A.** They stay at the office.

   _____ **B.** They stayed at the office.

8. _____ **A.** I work until midnight.

   _____ **B.** I worked until midnight.

Activity 17:   Practicing with a Partner

Work with a partner. Take turns reading one sentence from each pair of sentences in Activity 16. Write the letter of the sentence you hear. Remember that *A* is in the present tense and *B* is in the past tense. Check your answers with your partner.

1. _____   3. _____   5. _____   7. _____

2. _____   4. _____   6. _____   8. _____

Activity 18:   Linking with Consonants

Listen to Activity 18 on the tape. In the following pairs of words, the final sound of the first word is the same as the first sound of the second word. Notice how the speaker blends these words by not pronouncing the sounds separately, but by briefly lengthening, or holding, the sound. Repeat the words and then each sentence after the speaker.

1. next time   We'll do that next time.

2. bad day   We had a bad day.

3. some memos   He wrote some memos.

4. same mistake   They made the same mistake.

5. fair report   She wrote a fair report.

6. cheap pen   I bought a cheap pen.

Activity 19:   Listening to Linking

Listen to Activity 19 on the tape. Notice the way the speaker links certain sounds within each sentence. Repeat each sentence after the speaker.

1. She can never come here again.
2. That's the first time you've said it.
3. I wish she'd leave.
4. Her friend died.
5. The manager wrote several letters.
6. We bought two computers.
7. Paul went to sleep early.
8. The teacher ran to class.
9. Please continue with this activity.
10. I'll let you get to work.

Learning Strategies

Focusing on Grammar

To improve your grammar, you need to consider what kinds of grammatical mistakes you feel are serious.

Activity 20:   Assessing Grammar

1. Work individually or with a partner in the language lab or outside of class. Since this activity involves making a recording, be sure to have a blank thirty-minute audiotape. If a language lab is not available, you will need a cassette tape recorder and a microphone (if necessary).
2. Choose one of the situations presented in this or previous units. If you are working with a partner, you should each select different situations. Reread the situation, and, if necessary, take *brief* notes to help you remember the important facts. Then close your book. Spend a minute or

two planning how to explain this situation in your own words. Then, make a recording of your explanation.

3. Work with your instructor to choose one main grammar point to focus on: verb tenses, word order, etc.

4. Now work with a partner or a small group. Listen to your recording. Stop the tape every time you hear a mistake or think there is a problem in the grammar area that you have chosen. Work together to identify each mistake or problem, and work out a correct way of saying the same thing. Use the following chart to record your mistakes or problems. If necessary, use additional sheets of paper.

Mistake or Problem	Correction

5. If time is available, make another recording. Listen again to check for errors.

6. You may want to repeat this activity to focus on different grammar areas, such as word choice, pronunciation, and/or fluency. You may also want to make a recording to practice a class presentation. In this case, you can work alone or ask others to help you listen for and correct errors.

Cross-Cultural Communication

Considering Academic Dishonesty

Academic dishonesty includes lying, cheating, plagiarism,* and other types of dishonest conduct. Some situations are clear examples of academic dishonesty, such as when a student copies a classmate's answers during an exam. However, in other situations, it may be more difficult to identify academic dishonesty. In fact, some students may think that a certain activity is just helping a friend, while a teacher may regard it as academic dishonesty. Students from one culture might find that some activities that are acceptable in their country are unacceptable in another culture. These types of misunderstandings, of course, can cause students a great deal of trouble. Therefore, it is extremely important for everyone in class to have a clear understanding of what is considered to be academic dishonesty.

Activity 21:   Considering Academic Dishonesty

1. Work individually. Which of the following situations do you think are examples of academic dishonesty? In the column labeled *You*, write X if you think the action is an example of academic dishonesty or *Okay* if you think the action is acceptable.

    The word *source* in the chart is a general term referring to books, magazines, newspapers, computers, etc., that you might use to get information about a particular subject.

SITUATIONS	YOU	GROUP
A. Writing information for an exam on a small sheet of paper that you use during the exam.		
B. Writing information for an exam on a small sheet of paper and keeping it in your pocket, but not using it during the exam.		
C. Not covering your exam when you think another student is copying some of your answers.		
D. Working with a classmate on a homework assignment.		
E. Whispering one or two answers to a friend during a quiz.		

* *Plagiarism* means presenting another person's words or ideas as your own.

SITUATIONS	YOU	GROUP
F. Giving your homework assignment to another student to copy.		
G. Finding out exam questions from a friend who has already taken the same exam.		
H. Giving questions from an exam you have just finished to a friend who will take the exam later in the day. You aren't sure whether the teacher will give the same exam.		
I. Copying lecture or class notes from a classmate because you missed class.		
J. Discussing your ideas for a presentation with another student.		
K. Taking ideas and information for a presentation from one or more sources. You then put this information into your own words and do not give the name of your sources in your presentation.		
L. Using several sentences from a source, word-for-word, in a presentation. You give the name of your source but do not say that you are quoting the exact words.		
M. Using one or two sentences from a source, word-for-word, in a presentation. You do not say that you are quoting exact words from the source.		
N. Using information from sources as the main part of your presentation. You change a few words, leave out some sentences, and add a few sentences, so it is not exactly the same. You give the name of your source in your presentation.		
O. Having a native English speaker listen to your presentation for English class in advance to help you correct your mistakes.		

2. When everyone has finished, work in a small group to agree on a position. Write *X* or *Okay* in the column labeled *Group.*
3. When all the groups have finished, find out whether your teacher agrees with your answers. Then turn to the Answer Key on page 221 to see which actions were considered dishonest by a group of American professors.
4. For each case of academic dishonesty, what are the possible consequences?
5. You may want to discuss the problem of plagiarism with your teacher. Which actions in the chart are examples of plagiarism?

Unit 7

Solving a Problem

- Describe the scene in each photograph.
- How serious is the problem of drunk driving?
- Brainstorm ways of preventing or reducing the number of drunk driving accidents.
- Which ways do you feel are the most effective?

180

Listening Practice

Activity 1:   Evaluating Several Solutions

1. Work in a small group. Consider the problem of teenage violence in the United States. According to experts, teenage violence is caused by a complex mix of factors. Some of these causes include lack of parental supervision, family violence, excessive violence in the media, poverty, and easy access to guns. Clearly, it is difficult to find effective solutions to such a complex problem.

2. In this activity, you will hear several speakers discussing four solutions to the problem of teenage violence. These solutions all relate to one of the causes—lack of parental supervision. Before listening to the tape, review the section "Evaluating Solutions" in this unit. Be sure you understand the different criteria that are listed in the box "Judging Possible Solutions": cost, time, practicality, effectiveness, and acceptability.

3. Listen to Activity 1 on the tape. In each item, the speaker offers a possible solution. The other speakers then make comments or ask questions, using one of the following criteria: cost, time, practicality, effectiveness, or acceptability.

4. Put a check in front of the criterion that the speaker is discussing in each case.

A. *Suggested solution:* Offer classes to teach children how to handle anger.

1. _____ effectiveness   _____ time

2. _____ cost   _____ practicality

3. _____ acceptability   _____ cost

B. *Suggested solution:* Provide family counseling to families who need it.

1. _____ practicality   _____ time

2. _____ cost   _____ acceptability

3. _____ effectiveness   _____ time

C. *Suggested solution:* Provide recreational facilities for teenagers.

1. _____ cost   _____ effectiveness

2. _____ effectiveness   _____ time

3. _____ acceptability   _____ practicality

    D. *Suggested solution:* Offer classes to teach parents effective parenting skills.

      1. _____ acceptability   _____ cost

      2. _____ time   _____ practicality

      3. _____ effectiveness   _____ cost

      4. _____ time   _____ practicality

4. When everyone has finished, work in a small group or as a class to compare your answers.

Activity 2: Evaluating Parental Responsibility Laws

1. Work in a small group. Consider the following situation:

Situation. Children even younger than teenagers are starting to commit violent crimes in the United States. To fight these crimes, some states have passed parental responsibility laws. These laws hold parents responsible for crimes committed by their children. Judges may punish parents of guilty children by making them pay a fine or even sending them to jail.

2. What do you think are the advantages and disadvantages of these laws? Make a list on a separate sheet of paper.

3. Listen to Activity 2 on the tape. You will hear two people discussing parental responsibility laws. This discussion is broken down into separate segments. For each segment, put a check in front of the criterion that the speakers are considering.

    A. _____ acceptability   _____ time

    B. _____ cost   _____ practicality

    C. _____ practicality   _____ time

    D. _____ effectiveness   _____ cost

    E. _____ cost   _____ practicality

    F. _____ time   _____ effectiveness

4. When everyone has finished, work in a small group or as a class to compare your answers.

Communication Skills

Analyzing a Problem

For a problem-solving discussion to succeed, the participants must decide, "What exactly is the problem?" Group members may all describe the factual details of the situation in the same way, but they may also have very different ideas of the key issues involved. Clearly, people's views of the issues will strongly influence the types of solutions they offer. If group members do not agree on the nature of the problem, then they will have an even harder time agreeing on the best solution. Therefore, the group needs to examine the problem carefully before beginning to think of solutions.

1. The first step in examining a problem is to have one of the group members briefly review or summarize the situation.
2. Next, group members need to analyze the problem carefully by asking specific questions: *who, which, what, what kind of, where, when, why, how, how often, how many,* and *how long.* By discussing these questions, group members can come to a common understanding of the issues, causes, and nature of the problem. More specifically, it might help to consider the following questions:

A. What are the facts of the situation?

- What seems to be happening?
- Where is it taking place?
- Who is involved or affected?
- Who is responsible?

B. Very briefly, what is the basic conflict involved?
C. What is the history or background of the problem?

- Is this a new problem or an old one?
- When did it start?
- How has this problem developed?
- Have there been past efforts to deal with this problem? If so, what are they?

D. What are (or might be) the basic causes of this problem?
E. How serious or harmful is the problem?
F. What are (or might be) the effects of this problem?
G. What will (or might) happen if this problem continues?
H. Do we need more information? If so, where do we get it?

DEALING WITH A PROBLEM

Emphasizing a Point

It seems to me that the real issue is . . . .
I think the basic cause is . . . .
As far as I can see, the main problem is . . . .
In my opinion, the basic problem is . . . .

Activity 3:   Examining a Problem

1. Work in a small group. Analyze the following problem, using the questions presented in the previous section.

   Problem. The number of cars in a large city has increased dramatically over the past few years. City officials are concerned that it will soon be impossible to control the traffic jams. The city has a good bus and subway system, but people prefer driving to work. How can the number of people driving into the city be reduced?

2. When all the groups have finished, compare your ideas as a class.

Activity 4:   Analyzing a Problem of Your Choice

1. Work in a small group. Choose a real problem related to your school, job, community, country, etc. Analyze the problem using the questions presented in the previous section.
2. When all the groups have finished, take turns presenting each analysis to the class.

Gathering Information

This course has focused on using reasoning, observation, and personal experience to develop support for your ideas. In fact, the skills involved in gathering, recording, and using outside sources of information are beyond the scope of this text. However, in preparing a discussion or presentation on a complex topic or a controversial issue, you may want to do some research or interview people to gather more information. Clearly, the more you know about a problem, the more likely you are to develop effective solutions. Doing research and interviewing people can give you a better understanding of a problem—its causes, its background, its effects. Thus, you can add authority to your opinions by referring to relevant facts, specific details, expert opinions, etc. As you gather information, be sure to keep a careful record of all the sources that you use. Then, you will be able to indicate the source of any quotations or summaries by using such phrases as, "Ac-

cording to . . ." or "John Smith, a well-known expert in the field, believes that . . . ."

Doing Research

The best place to begin doing research is in the library. If you are not sure how to use the resources in the library, you can ask one of the library staff for help. Most libraries catalog their books in one of two ways: in card catalogs or in computer catalogs. You will need to find out how to locate books in your particular library. For a source of general information, you should become familiar with *The Readers' Guide to Periodical Literature*, which is an index of many popular magazines. In addition, a librarian can help you compile a list of sources on a particular subject by using a computerized data base, if available. If you would like to know more about research than is presented here, you can do the following activity.

Activity 5: Learning More about Research

Work individually or in a small group to prepare reports on some of the following topics:

1. What type of catalog system is used in your library—a card catalog or a computer catalog? Briefly, how does this system work?
2. How can you locate information using the card or computer catalog?
3. What kind of book classification system is used in your library—the Library of Congress system, the Dewey decimal system, or another system? How does this system work?
4. How can you locate books on the shelves of the library using the catalog?
5. What is a periodical index? a newspaper index? What are some of the most useful indexes in your library?
6. How can you locate information on specific subjects using periodical indexes?
7. How can you locate specific articles using periodical indexes?
8. What are the different kinds of reference materials found in the library? Briefly, explain the type of information you can find in a general encyclopedia, a specialized encyclopedia, a biographical register, an atlas, an almanac, and a dictionary.
9. How can you use computer data bases (if available) to get information?
10. What other resources does your library have, such as pamphlets, records, tapes, compact discs, videos, or films?

Interviewing Others

In addition to doing library research, you may also obtain information by interviewing experts in the field. These experts may be teachers, professors, government officials, or business executives—anyone who has experience in your field. In some situations, you may simply want to find out the different viewpoints that people have on a particular topic.

Evaluating Solutions

People often work in committees or groups to solve problems. In a problem-solving group, it is important to take the time to look at the advantages and disadvantages of each possible solution. As discussed in earlier units, you must consider the rights, obligations, values, and possible consequences that are involved in a particular solution. When judging a particular solution, you might also consider the cost, time, practicality, effectiveness, and acceptability involved. Of course, these criteria vary in importance according to the specific situation.

JUDGING POSSIBLE SOLUTIONS

Getting the Facts

Who . . . ?
What . . . ?
Where . . . ?
When . . . ?
Why . . . ?
How . . . ?

Cost

Can we afford this solution?
Is the solution worth the cost?

Time

How long will it take to get results?
Is the solution worth the time it will take to get results?

Practicality

How easy will it be to put this plan into effect?

How $\left\{ \begin{array}{l} \text{workable} \\ \text{practical} \end{array} \right\}$ is this plan?

Do we have the necessary $\left\{ \begin{array}{l} \text{resources?} \\ \text{people?} \\ \text{facilities?} \end{array} \right.$

Will this solution require $\left\{ \begin{array}{l} \text{making many changes?} \\ \text{passing new laws?} \\ \text{doing a lot of paperwork?} \end{array} \right.$

Effectiveness

Does this plan really deal with the causes of the problem?

Will this solution $\left\{ \begin{array}{l} \text{really solve the problem?} \\ \text{improve the situation?} \end{array} \right.$

Acceptability

Will everyone involved $\left\{ \begin{array}{l} \text{accept} \\ \text{agree to} \end{array} \right\}$ this plan?

People use the criteria of cost, time, practicality, effectiveness, and acceptability as well as rights, obligations, values, and possible consequences in analyzing a proposed solution. Of course, it is also necessary to give reasons and/or specific details to support your opinions. For example, if you say a plan is "impractical," then you have to explain specifically how or why it is impractical. The following chart includes some expressions you can use in opposing or supporting a particular solution.

CRITERIA	MAKING OBJECTIONS	SHOWING SUPPORT
Cost	It's too expensive. We can't afford it. It isn't worth the cost.	The cost is reasonable. We can afford it. It's worth the cost.
Time	It will take too long to get results. It isn't worth the time.	We'll get immediate results. It's worth the time it will take.

Practicality	It's { impractical.
	        unworkable.
	It's too complicated.
	We don't have the necessary
	    resources, such as . . . .
		It's { practical.
		        workable.
		It's easy to put into effect.
		We can easily get the necessary
		    resources, such as . . . .

Effectiveness	It won't solve the real problem. It will make the situation worse.	It will solve the problem. It will improve the situation.
Acceptability	People will never accept this plan because . . . . People won't agree to it.	Everyone will accept this plan. People will agree to it.

Rights, obligations,
values
	It's { unfair.
	        unethical.
	        dishonest.
	        illegal.
		It's { fair.
		        ethical.
		        honest.
		        legal.

Possible
consequences
	The disadvantages outweigh the
	    advantages.
	The consequences are just too
	    harmful.
		The advantages outweigh the
		    disadvantages.
		The consequences are more
		    beneficial than harmful.

In discussing a solution to a problem, you need to be able to predict possible objections that others (inside or outside your group) might have. By thinking of these objections in advance, you can develop counterarguments to support your own ideas. You may also be able to adjust the solution to avoid these objections.

Activity 6: Evaluating Solutions

1. Work in a small group. Discuss one of the following situations. Spend a few minutes analyzing the problem before considering the suggested solution. Then use a separate sheet of paper to list as many possible *objections* to this solution that your group can develop. Do not compare the solution to one that you think is better. Focus only on the solution that is mentioned.

   A. *Situation.* The U.S. Surgeon General has warned the public about the hazards of drinking alcohol while pregnant. Drinking can damage the fetus. Furthermore, babies born to mothers who drink during their pregnancy may suffer from physical abnormalities or lowered intelligence.

   Suggested Solution. State officials are considering a law to jail pregnant women who refuse to stop drinking.

   B. *Situation.* City officials are alarmed at the growing problem of gang violence. According to the mayor, "In the past year we have seen a dramatic increase in gang violence and crimes committed by young people." Just last week, five teenagers were killed in gang-related incidents.

   Suggested Solution. The mayor has announced plans to impose a curfew on teenagers. This curfew will require teenagers 16 years old and younger to be off the streets and at home by 10:00 P.M. After 10:00, police have the right to question and arrest any young person who is out.

2. When all the groups have finished, share your ideas as a class.

Following Steps in Problem Solving

Discussion groups are most efficient when they follow a logical step-by-step procedure in problem solving. The most common procedure that effective groups use is the problem-solution pattern of problem solving. Following this pattern, the group first analyzes the problem and then moves on to the solution stage of the discussion. If all group members are familiar with this pattern, the discussion will be much more organized. The problem-solution pattern includes the following steps:

1. *Defining and analyzing the problem:* The group needs to develop a clear statement of the problem to be solved. Once the problem is defined, the group can begin to analyze it. The purpose of this step is to bring out different viewpoints and facts so that everyone understands all the factors involved in the problem.
2. *Brainstorming solutions:* Next, members brainstorm ideas to develop a list of all possible solutions to the problem, without stopping to judge the quality of the ideas.
3. *Choosing the most likely, most effective, or most interesting solutions:* When the group has finished brainstorming solutions, members can choose

three or four solutions to discuss in more detail. These solutions are those that generally seem to be the most likely, the most effective, or the most interesting. At this stage, the group can also try to think of ways of combining two or more solutions.

4. *Considering each solution:* Now the group is ready to discuss the proposed solutions, one by one. Considering a solution actually involves two stages: clarifying and evaluating.

   A. *Clarifying:* Group members work together to clarify how each solution might work by discussing such questions as:

      - How exactly will we do it?
      - Who will be responsible for doing it?
      - When and where will we do it?
      - Who will pay for it?
      - What resources will we need?

      Keep in mind that it is *not* the responsibility of the person who suggested a solution to answer all these questions.

   B. *Evaluating:* After the group has clarified the solution, members can begin evaluating it according to the criteria that apply, such as cost, time, practicality, effectiveness, possible consequences, etc. These criteria give the group a common basis for judging the advantages and disadvantages of possible solutions. After the group has carefully considered one solution, the leader can bring up the next one for discussion. Of course, members should consider all of the proposed solutions before making a final decision.

5. *Selecting the best solution:* After discussing all of the solutions, group members can compare their advantages and disadvantages. Clearly, the group should choose the solution or combination of solutions that has the most advantages and the fewest disadvantages. The group should try to reach a consensus on the best solution to the problem.

DEALING WITH SUGGESTIONS

Suggesting Action

Perhaps we could . . . .
We might try . . . .
Why don't we . . . ?
What about . . . ?
How about . . . ?

Accepting a Suggestion

> Yes, of course.
> That's a great idea.
> Yes, why don't we try that?

Expressing Doubts

> Well, I'm not really sure.
> I don't know—maybe.
> Well, . . . maybe.

Rejecting a Suggestion

> I'm not sure that will work because . . . .
> I'm afraid that might not be such a good idea because . . . .

Activity 7:   Brainstorming Possible Solutions

1. Work in a small group. Choose one of the following situations. Spend ten minutes brainstorming possible solutions to the problem. List your ideas on a separate sheet of paper. Remember that the goal of brainstorming is to produce as many ideas as possible. Be sure not to judge any ideas that people mention.

   A. *Situation.* Police officials in this city are frustrated by the increasing numbers of cars that are stolen. Many of these cars are parked directly in front of the owner's house. How can the number of stolen cars be reduced?

   B. *Situation.* Some international students at this Canadian university are frustrated because it seems so difficult for them to make friends with Canadians. How can they meet more Canadians?

2. At the end of ten minutes, stop brainstorming.

   • Cross out any ideas that do not seem to fit.
   • Spend a few more minutes adding any new ideas that come to mind.

3. When all the groups have finished, share your ideas as a class.

To choose the best solution to a particular problem, you have to compare the strengths and weaknesses of all the solutions that are offered. The following box lists some expressions that you may find useful in comparing solutions.

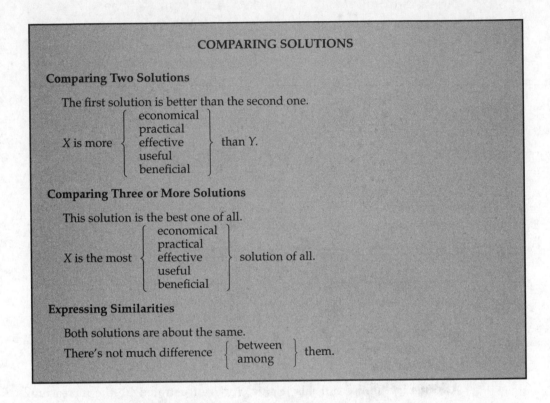

COMPARING SOLUTIONS

Comparing Two Solutions

The first solution is better than the second one.

X is more { economical / practical / effective / useful / beneficial } than Y.

Comparing Three or More Solutions

This solution is the best one of all.

X is the most { economical / practical / effective / useful / beneficial } solution of all.

Expressing Similarities

Both solutions are about the same.

There's not much difference { between / among } them.

Activity 8:   Solving a Problem

1. Work in a small group. Consider the following situation:

   Situation. Dr. Martha Kenrick has been a highly respected university professor in the Department of English for the past fifteen years. She has published many articles and has always received outstanding teaching evaluations from her students. Several months ago, she won a prize for an article she wrote. She was paid $1,000, and the article was published in a magazine. Now university officials have discovered that Dr. Kenrick copied two paragraphs of her article word-for-word from a paper a student had written as a class assignment. Dr. Kenrick did not give this student credit as the source of her information. She has apologized and promised that this will never happen again.

2. Imagine that members of your group are a university committee that includes students, faculty members, and administration officials. Spend ten minutes brainstorming possible ways of dealing with this situation. List all the ideas that you can think of on a separate sheet of paper.

3. At the end of ten minutes, stop brainstorming.

   • Cross out any ideas that do not seem to fit.
   • Spend a few more minutes adding any new ideas that come to mind.

4. Now select five of the best or most likely solutions to add to the list below:

   A. University officials should fire Professor Kenrick.

   B. _____

   C. _____

   D. _____

   E. _____

   F. _____

5. Work as a group to compare the solutions. Select the one with the most advantages and the fewest disadvantages. Be prepared to support your decision with reasons.
6. When all the groups have finished, share your ideas as a class.

Activity 9: Dealing with Problems

1. Work in a small group. Discuss one or more of the following situations. Follow the steps in problem solving to choose the best solution to each problem. Be sure to provide reasons to support your decision.

A. *Situation.* Managers in a large automobile factory are very concerned about the high rate of absenteeism among the workers. One of the main problems seems to be that many workers are absent on days just before or after the weekend.

Group Decision. How can this high absentee rate be reduced?

B. *Situation.* A university professor who teaches an 8:00 A.M. class four times per week feels very frustrated because many students regularly arrive ten or fifteen minutes late. The university policy is that professors cannot consider lateness or absences in determining final course grades. Therefore, the professor cannot lower students' grades simply because they are late.

Group Decision. How can the number of tardy students be reduced?

C. *Situation.* Workers in a large manufacturing company have two fifteen-minute breaks per day, but they have been stretching these breaks to last up to thirty minutes each. Company executives say that these extended breaks are causing the business to lose hundreds of work hours per year. Workers complain that the factory work is so boring that they need longer breaks.

Group Decision. How should the company deal with this problem?

D. *Situation.* After three weeks of class, international students in an English-language program at a university are very dissatisfied with their professor. He doesn't explain the material, doesn't seem prepared, and doesn't answer their questions.

Group Decision. How should the students deal with this situation?

E. *Situation.* A university professor strongly believes that an EFL student has copied entire sections word-for-word from a book into her final research paper. The writing in these sections includes complex grammatical structures, advanced vocabulary, and absolutely no errors—completely different from the student's usual work. The student, however, did not credit any source for these sections and says the work is original, not copied. The professor, unfortunately, cannot locate the source of the material.

Group Decision. How should the professor deal with this situation?

2. Your teacher or other observers may use the Group Discussion Evaluation II Form in Appendix A.
3. When all the groups have finished, compare your ideas as a class.

Activity 10:   Developing Your Own Situation

1. Work in a small group. Choose a problem in class, at work, or in the community. Try to pick a problem that is not too complex.
2. Write a brief explanation of the situation in one or two paragraphs. Be sure that the conflict is stated clearly.
3. Write a clear statement of the discussion question or decision to be made. Use the problem situations presented in this unit as models.
4. Work with your instructor to make any necessary changes in the case.
5. Work in your group to try to solve this problem, following the steps of problem solving.
6. You may want to trade problems with other groups.
7. When all the groups have finished, share your ideas as a class.

Pronunciation Practice

Intonation Patterns in Questions

Stress gives English its rhythm, while intonation provides its melody. *Intonation* is the rising and falling of your voice when you are speaking. It is this rising and falling that make the melody or tune. English speakers generally use one of two basic intonation patterns when asking questions, depending on the type of question.

Rising intonation is usually used at the end of yes-no questions. This means that the pitch is raised on the last syllable or word that is stressed in the sentence. This high pitch, then, is maintained to the end of the question.

Activity 11:   Listening to Questions with Rising Intonation

Listen to Activity 11 on the tape. Can you hear the way the pitch rises at the end of each question? Repeat after the speaker, trying to imitate the rising intonation pattern. Keep repeating the questions until they sound natural to you.

1. Is that right?
2. Are we ready to begin?
3. Was that legal?
4. Do we all agree?
5. Does everybody understand the problem?
6. Did you summarize the situation?
7. Has everyone made a decision?
8. Have you all finished?
9. Will this improve the situation?
10. Can we afford this plan?
11. Should we try a different solution?
12. May I ask you a question?

Activity 12:   Listening to Intonation

People use intonation to indicate whether they are asking a question or making a statement. Listen to Activity 12 on the tape. For each item, the speaker will first ask a question and then make a statement, using the same word(s). Listen and repeat, trying to imitate the intonation that the speaker uses.

1. Ready?   Ready.
2. Now?   Now.
3. Okay?   Okay.
4. Right?   Right.
5. Wrong?   Wrong.
6. Yes?   Yes.
7. No?   No.
8. Definitely?   Definitely.
9. Really?   Really.
10. At work?   At work.

Activity 13:   Distinguishing Questions from Statements

Listen to Activity 13 on the tape. The speaker will say each item twice. In each blank, write *Q* if the item sounds like a question or *S* if it sounds like a statement.

1. _____	5. _____	9. _____	13. _____
2. _____	6. _____	10. _____	14. _____
3. _____	7. _____	11. _____	15. _____
4. _____	8. _____	12. _____	16. _____

Falling intonation is used for information questions, such as *who, what, what kind of, which, where, when, why,* and *how.* This means that the pitch rises on the last stressed syllable in the sentence, and then falls on the rest of the unstressed syllables or words.

Activity 14:   Listening to Questions with Falling Intonation

Listen to Activity 14 on the tape. Can you hear the way the pitch changes from high to low in the following questions? Repeat after the speaker, trying to follow the same falling intonation pattern. Keep repeating the questions until they sound natural to you.

1. Who's your boss?
2. What's your opinion?
3. What do you mean?
4. What was the problem?
5. Which solution is the best?
6. Where did they hold the meeting?
7. When should we begin?
8. Why do you think that?
9. How do you spell that?
10. How long did the meeting last?
11. How much was the bill?
12. How many people have you met?

Activity 15: Identifying Rising or Falling Intonation

Listen to Activity 15 on the tape. The speaker will say each question twice. Listen carefully to hear what kind of intonation the speaker uses. In each blank below, write *R* if you hear rising intonation or *F* if you hear falling intonation.

1. _____   5. _____   9. _____   13. _____

2. _____   6. _____   10. _____   14. _____

3. _____   7. _____   11. _____   15. _____

4. _____   8. _____   12. _____   16. _____

Learning Strategies

Assessing Your Progress

Take some time to consider how much progress you have made in this course by completing the following activity.

Activity 16: Assessing Your Progress

1. How much progress do you feel you have made in this course? Use the following key to complete the chart:

   + = I feel satisfied with the progress I have made.
   √ = I have made some progress, but I still need a lot more practice.
   − = I still have serious weaknesses in this area.

SKILLS	PROGRESS
A. Participation in class	
B. Participation in conversations	
C. Participation in group discussions	
D. Giving oral presentations	
E. Pronunciation	
F. Fluency	
G. Listening comprehension	
H. Feeling confident about speaking	

2. Work in a small group. Discuss the following:

   • In which skills have members of your group made the most progress?
   • Which skills still seem to be the weakest?

3. Spend a few minutes looking through your textbook. Think about the types of activities you have done in this course. In your group, discuss the following:

   • Which activities have you found the most useful?
   • Which activities have you enjoyed the most?

4. When all the groups have finished, share your ideas as a class.

Activity 17:   Planning Strategies for Improvement

1. Work individually. Make a list of the ways that you plan to continue trying to improve your speaking and listening skills in English.

   A. _____

   B. _____

   C. _____

   D. _____

   E. _____

2. When everyone has finished, work in a small group or as a class to share your ideas.

Evaluating the Course

Complete the Final Course Evaluation Form in Appendix D.

Cross-Cultural Communication

Considering Social Situations

Different cultures have different rules for social interaction. Behavior that is acceptable or polite in one culture may seem unacceptable or rude in another.

Activity 18:   Discussing Social Situations

1. Work in a small group. Consider each of the following social situations. For each situation, answer these questions:

   - Do you think that the behavior is appropriate/polite in the United States? If certain behavior seems inappropriate/impolite, what social rule has been broken?
   - Is the behavior appropriate/polite in your culture? If it seems inappropriate/impolite, what social rule has been broken?

   A. *Situation.* Mr. and Mrs. Lawrence, an American couple, have invited several international students to their home for dinner. When the students accept the invitation, Mrs. Lawrence tells them to come around 6:00. The students arrive at 7:30.

   Discussion. What do you think about the students' behavior?

   B. *Situation.* Maria's colleague at work has invited several people from the office to lunch at her home on Saturday afternoon. Ten minutes before it's time for Maria to leave, two of her good friends drop by the house unexpectedly. Maria hasn't seen them in some time, so they spend twenty minutes talking. Maria then says, "Why don't you come with me to lunch?" Her friends accept and go with Maria to her colleague's home for lunch.

Discussion. What do you think about Maria's behavior and the behavior of her friends?

C. *Situation*. Ms. Flynn, a university professor, has invited her students to her house to celebrate the end of the semester. She arranges to have the dinner on a night when everyone is free. Ms. Flynn is very pleased that all eighteen students say that they will be able to come. Five students, however, do not show up for the dinner. The next day in class, they say they couldn't come because they were busy.

Discussion. What do you think about the students' behavior?

D. *Situation*. On Monday, Mike Barrett invited several colleagues to his house for dinner on Saturday night. At the time he invited everyone, one colleague, Ed Galloway, said he wasn't sure whether he could come. On Thursday Mike talks to Ed again. Ed says he still isn't sure, but that he will try to come to dinner on Saturday.

Discussion. What do you think about Ed's behavior?

E. *Situation*. Sami has planned to meet a classmate in front of the library at 2:00. On the way to the library, however, Sami runs into some friends. He hasn't seen them for several weeks, so they have a lot of news to discuss. Sami arrives at the library at 2:30.

Discussion. What do you think about Sami's behavior?

2. When all the groups have finished, share your ideas as a class.
3. Turn to the Answer Key on page 221 to see some typical responses of people in the United States.

Appendix A

Evaluation Forms

Unit 1:   Class Participation Evaluation Form

Write the name of each student in the left column. In the middle column, put a check each time the person volunteers a comment or question. After the activity, write the total number of each student's contributions in the column labeled *Total*.

STUDENTS	CONTRIBUTIONS	TOTAL

Unit 2:   Conversation Evaluation Form

Speaker A: _____   Overall rating: _____

Speaker B: _____   Overall rating: _____

Use the following key to evaluate the conversation skills of the speakers:

+ = very good   √ = satisfactory   − = needs more practice

CONVERSATION SKILLS	SPEAKER A	SPEAKER B
1. Looks directly at the other speaker during the conversation		
2. Takes an equal part in the conversation		
3. Encourages the other speaker verbally and/or nonverbally		
4. Takes initiative by making comments and/or asking questions		

Unit 3:   Presentation Evaluation I Form

Speaker: _____ Time: _____

Topic: _____ Grade or Rating: _____

Use the following key to evaluate the presentation skills of each speaker:

+ = very good   √ = satisfactory   − = needs more practice

A.   Delivery

_____ Maintained eye contact with listeners in all parts of the room

_____ Spoke loudly and clearly

_____ Spoke in a natural, conversational manner

_____ Used effective posture, movement, and gestures

_____ Used notes effectively (if applicable)

B.   Communicative ability

_____ Pronunciation was clear

_____ Spoke fluently, without too much hesitation or repetition

_____ Grammar and vocabulary choices were reasonably accurate

C.   Content

_____ Fulfilled assignment

_____ Met time limit

Unit 4: Group Discussion Evaluation I Form

Speaker A: _____   Speaker B: _____

Speaker C: _____   Speaker D: _____

Topic: _____

Put a check in the chart below each time you observe a speaker display one of the following discussion skills. You can then use this information to help evaluate the group.

DISCUSSION SKILLS	SPEAKER A	SPEAKER B	SPEAKER C	SPEAKER D
1. Contributes ideas				
2. Asks questions				

Use the following key to evaluate the group as a whole:

    + = very good   √ = satisfactory   – = needs more practice

_____ **A.** *Clarity:* All group members spoke loudly and clearly.

_____ **B.** *Participation:* All group members contributed ideas and took equal part in the discussion.

_____ **C.** *Pace:* The discussion moved along at the right speed, without long pauses between speakers.

Unit 5:   Presentation Evaluation II Form

Speaker: _____ Time: _____

Topic: _____ Grade or Rating: _____

Use the following key to evaluate the presentation skills of each speaker:

+ = very good   √ = satisfactory   − = needs more practice

A. Delivery

_____ Maintained eye contact with listeners in all parts of the room

_____ Spoke loudly and clearly

_____ Spoke in a natural, conversational manner

_____ Used effective posture, movement, and gestures

_____ Used notes effectively (if applicable)

B. Communicative ability

_____ Pronunciation was clear

_____ Spoke fluently, without too much hesitation or repetition

_____ Grammar and vocabulary choices were reasonably accurate

C. Content

_____ Fulfilled assignment

_____ Met time limit

_____ Developed topic with sufficient reasons, examples, and details

_____ Chose a topic that was appropriate for the audience

D. Organization

_____ Effective introduction

_____ Logical development of ideas

_____ Clear transitions

_____ Effective conclusion

Unit 6:   Individual Evaluation of Group Members Form

Speaker A: _____   Speaker B: _____

Speaker C: _____   Speaker D: _____

Topic: _____

Put a check in the chart each time you observe a speaker display one of the following discussion skills. Then use the following key to evaluate each group member:

   + = very good   √ = satisfactory   – = needs more practice

DISCUSSION SKILLS	SPEAKER A	SPEAKER B	SPEAKER C	SPEAKER D
1. Contributes ideas				
2. Asks questions				
3. Encourages other speakers verbally and/or nonverbally				
Individual Rating				

Unit 7:   Group Discussion Evaluation II Form

Speaker A: _____   Speaker B: _____

Speaker C: _____   Speaker D: _____

Topic: _____

Put a check in the chart below each time you observe a speaker display one of the following discussion skills. You can then use this information to evaluate the group.

DISCUSSION SKILLS	SPEAKER A	SPEAKER B	SPEAKER C	SPEAKER D
1. Contributes ideas				
2. Asks questions				

Use the following key to evaluate the group as a whole:

+ = very good   √ = satisfactory   – = needs more practice

_____ **A.** *Clarity:* All group members spoke loudly and clearly.

_____ **B.** *Participation:* All group members contributed ideas and took equal part in the discussion.

_____ **C.** *Pace:* The discussion moved along at the right speed, without long pauses between speakers.

_____ **D.** *Problem Solving:* The discussion moved in an organized, logical way toward the final decision.

_____ **E.** *Leader Control:* The leader effectively guided the discussion, not taking too much or too little control.

Appendix B

Subjects

Keep in mind that you will have to narrow these broad subject areas into specific topics to make them suitable for a presentation. Remember also that these are only suggestions; many other subjects would also make interesting topics.

1. *Educational/school issues:* Cheating, computers in the classroom, discipline in the classroom, free university education, good teachers, learning, motivating students, pass/fail grading, responsibilities of college students

2. *Professional/work issues:* Choosing a career, flextime, hiring the physically handicapped, home computers, mandatory retirement, military service, moonlighting, offices of the future, part-time jobs, polygraph testing of employees, three-day weekends, women's opportunities

3. *Family/friends:* Adoption, arranged marriages, caring for an aging parent, divorce, extended families, friendship, limiting the size of families, living together before marriage, nuclear families, qualities of a friend, single parents

4. *Medical/health issues:* Adolescence, alcoholism, animal rights, children with AIDS, death with dignity, depression, diet and exercise, dreams, folk medicine, hypnosis to stop smoking, insomnia, mandatory drug testing, memory, mental health, nutrition, organ transplants, overpopulation, passive smoke, sleep, stress, teen suicide, terminally ill patients, vegetarianism

5. *Sports/recreation:* Banning violent sports, censorship of rock music, leisure time, sports for the handicapped, steroid use by athletes

6. *Science/technology:* Acid rain, alternative sources of energy, deforestation, electronic mail, endangered species, energy conservation, laptop com-

puters, lasers, noise pollution, nuclear energy, recycling, saving the whale (dolphin), saving rain forests, scarcity of natural resources, solar energy, space travel, using animals in medical research, wind energy

7. *Social issues:* Abortion, adoption, advertising, advertising aimed at children, aging, animal rights, begging/panhandling, capital punishment, care of the elderly, censorship, child abuse, cigarette advertising, consumer protection, culture shock, day care, drug abuse, drunk driving, gambling, gangs, gun control, homelessness, illiteracy, legalizing drugs, life in the city, military service, minorities, muggings, nursing homes, poverty, prison reform, racism, rape, retirement, sex discrimination, spouse abuse, tourism, violence, violence in the media, women in combat, women's rights

8. *Cross-cultural issues:* Art, customs, dance, dating, death, economy, education, entertainment, family, food, government, history, holidays, housing, labor, leisure, marriage, music, nonverbal communication, politics, religion, sense of time, sports, traditions, values, youth

9. *Miscellaneous:* Abandoning pets, ESP, litter, lotteries, military service, natural disasters, public transportation, self-defense, skyscrapers, television, UFOs

10. *Processes:* How food is turned into energy, how glass is made, how paper is manufactured

11. *How to do or make something:* Avoiding jet lag, being safe in a city, handling household emergencies, preparing a favorite dish, staying on a budget

Appendix C

Guidelines for Developing an Oral Presentation

1. Assess the speaking situation

   A. Select your subject
   B. Narrow your subject to a topic
   C. Analyze your audience
   D. Make sure you meet all the guidelines

2. Explore your topic

   A. Listing
   B. Clustering

3. Organize your ideas

   A. Make a working outline

   - A tree diagram; or
   - An informal outline

   B. Brainstorm more ideas to provide strong support

   - Explanations
   - Examples
   - Anecdotes
   - Scenarios
   - Concrete details
   - Reasons
   - Consequences

    C. Gather any additional information you may need
    D. Reorganize ideas or change the focus of the presentation, if necessary
    E. Prepare the introduction and conclusion
    F. Write a final outline

4. Prepare

    A. Review your outline
    B. Write brief presentation notes on note cards
    C. Use a dictionary or teacher assistance to check on the pronunciation of any new or unfamiliar vocabulary words
    D. Practice giving your presentation in advance to check timing and gain confidence

Appendix D

Final Course Evaluation Form

Student Questionnaire

Your answers to the following questions will help your teacher improve future courses, so please give your honest opinions. You should follow your teacher's instructions in marking your answers. You may either: (1) write your answers on a separate sheet of paper or (2) write your answers on a photocopy of this evaluation. In any case, you do *not* have to put your name on the paper.

As you answer these questions, don't forget the difference between the words *very* and *too*. For example, when you say something is "*very* easy," you simply mean that it is quite easy or especially easy. However, when you say that something is "*too* easy," you mean that it is easier than you want or need it to be, which has a negative meaning.

Part 1

1. In general, the course was _____.

   A. very good
   B. average/satisfactory
   C. poor

2. The teacher was _____.

   A. very good
   B. average/satisfactory
   C. poor

216

3. The textbook was _____.

   A. very useful
   B. somewhat useful
   C. not useful

4. The textbook was _____.

   A. very interesting
   B. somewhat interesting
   C. not interesting

5. The level of the class was _____.

   A. too easy
   B. about right
   C. too difficult

6. Did the teacher give everyone in class an equal chance to participate?

   A. almost always
   B. usually
   C. sometimes
   D. almost never

7. How often did you personally speak in class?

   A. frequently
   B. sometimes
   C. almost never

8. The teacher corrected the students' mistakes _____.

   A. too often
   B. about right
   C. not enough

9. The general mood of the class was _____.

   A. too serious
   B. about right
   C. too much joking

10. When you worked in a group (without the teacher listening), how often did you speak English?

   A. almost always
   B. usually
   C. sometimes
   D. almost never

11. Did you understand what the teacher said?

   A. almost always
   B. usually
   C. sometimes
   D. almost never

12. How did you feel about the way the teacher graded or evaluated you?

   A. It was generally fair.
   B. It was unfair.
   C. I did not understand the way the teacher evaluated me.

13. Did the teacher's explanations help you understand the information?

   A. almost always
   B. usually
   C. sometimes
   D. almost never

14. Working with a partner in class was _____.

   A. very useful
   B. somewhat useful
   C. not useful

15. Small group discussions in class were _____.

   A. very useful
   B. somewhat useful
   C. not useful

16. Giving oral presentations in class was _____.

   A. very useful
   B. somewhat useful
   C. not useful

17. The listening activities were _____.

   A. very useful
   B. somewhat useful
   C. not useful

18. The pronunciation activities were _____.

   A. very useful
   B. somewhat useful
   C. not useful

19. In general, do you feel that your speaking and listening skills improved in this course?

    A. They improved a lot.
    B. They improved a little.
    C. They didn't improve.

20. Approximately how many classes have you missed?

    A. 0–2
    B. 3–5
    C. 6–8
    D. 9 or more

Part 2

As you answer these questions, you may want to look through this textbook. Please feel free to explain your answers.

1. Which units did you find the most useful?

_____

_____

2. Do you think the teacher should skip any units in the future?

_____

_____

3. Do you have any comments on this course or suggestions for future courses?

_____

_____

_____

_____

_____

_____

_____

Answer Key

Unit 1, Activity 15: Considering Appropriate Behavior

A. Stay seated, look at the teacher, and say, "Good morning."
B. Walk in quietly, sit down in the nearest seat, and explain to the teacher after class.
C. All of the behaviors listed are usually *not* acceptable.

Unit 5, Activity 20: Comparing Behavior

A. First speak with other students, then go to the teacher. If this does not improve the situation, then go to the director.
B. Make an appointment to speak with the teacher outside of class.
C. Explain the situation to the teacher before class and ask for a postponement.
D. After exchanging greetings for a minute or two, explain the situation and ask her to write the letter.

Unit 6, Activity 21: Considering Academic Dishonesty

Many American professors believe that the following items are cases of academic dishonesty:

A, B, C, E, F, G, H, K, L, M, N

Items K, L, M, and N may need further explanation from your teacher.

Unit 7, Activity 18: Discussing Social Situations

A. Generally, people in the United States expect guests to arrive on time (but not early) for a dinner invitation. For many people, it is acceptable to arrive fifteen or twenty minutes after the designated time. If guests are going to be later than that, it is polite to call the host to explain the delay. Therefore, to an American, it would seem rude for these students to arrive so late.
B. Maria should have explained the situation and apologized to her friends

B. Maria should have explained the situation and apologized to her friends for having to leave, but she should not have invited them to the lunch. Since she did not do this, however, her friends should have understood the situation, refused her invitation, and left right away to allow Maria to get to the party on time. In the United States, it is not generally acceptable to bring uninvited people to a social gathering without asking the host's permission. However, guests need to be careful about putting the host in a difficult position by calling at the last minute to ask whether they may bring someone else. To be polite, the host might say yes, yet he or she might feel annoyed because the food was planned for a specific number of people.

C. This behavior might seem very rude. After the students accepted the invitation, it was not acceptable to say they couldn't come to dinner because they were "busy." If they couldn't attend because of an unexpected problem at the last minute, the students should have called to explain their situation. They also needed to give a more specific reason than that they were "busy."

D. Mike might think that Ed really does not want to come to his house for dinner. Mike might also think that Ed is waiting for a better or more interesting invitation for Saturday night. Therefore, Ed's uncertainty (with no explanation) seems rude. Ed should either accept the invitation and go to dinner, or politely refuse the invitation with a reason.

E. It was rude for Sami to have kept his classmate waiting for half an hour. That is a long time to keep someone waiting outside a building.